AGING IN PLACE: USING UNIVERSAL DESIGN

DISCOVER HOW TO CREATE YOUR FUTURE ACCESSIBLE HOME YOU WILL NEVER HAVE TO LEAVE

KATE BIGALK

Dedication

I would like to dedicate this book to my mom, stepdad, sister, brother-in-law, nieces, my stepbrother, and his family, my stepsister and her family, and to ALL of my other family members and ALL of my friends (who are like family) who have always encouraged me to believe in myself.

Thanks for all of the memories to my dad and brother in heaven. Thanks for all of the rainbows you send to us!

TABLE OF CONTENTS

PART I

INTRODUCTION

1. WHO WANTS TO AGE IN PLACE? WHY
   TAKE MY ADVICE?   3
2. THE REASON WHY YOU REALLY NEED AN
   ACCESSIBLE HOME   10

PART II

**UNIVERSAL DESIGN AND AGING IN
PLACE**

3. WHAT EVERYONE OUGHT TO KNOW
   ABOUT UNIVERSAL DESIGN   19
   Seven Real-Life Examples of Universal Design   23
   Incorporating Universal Design into a Home   26

4. OK, SO. HOW DO I AGE IN PLACE?   28

PART III

**AGING IN PLACE: AROUND
YOUR HOME**

5. WHAT YOU NEED TO KNOW ABOUT AN
   ACCESSIBLE HOME EXTERIOR AND
   ENTRANCE   37
   The Garage   55

6. CRACKING THE ACCESSIBLE LIVING
   ROOM CODE   61

7. A KITCHEN FOR EVERYONE   73
   Hazards in the Kitchen   73
   The Location of the Kitchen   75
   Kitchen Lighting   76
   Kitchen Cabinets   80

Kitchen Countertop   81

Kitchen Appliances   83

14 TYPES OF KITCHEN SINKS   86

Refrigerator And Freezer   98

9 Types of Dishwashers   103

Safety in the Kitchen   106

8. EVERYTHING YOU WANTED TO KNOW ABOUT DESIGNING THE MAIN BEDROOM AND CLOSET AND WERE AFRAID TO ASK   110

Second-floor main bedroom   111

Bedroom Safety   112

The Bed and Other Furniture In The Main Bedroom   113

Flooring   115

Main Bedroom Lighting   116

The Main Bedroom Closet   120

9. WHAT YOU CAN DO ABOUT DESIGNING AN ACCESSIBLE MAIN BEDROOM ENSUITE BATHROOM RIGHT NOW   124

Bathroom Design   125

Tubs and Showers   127

Toilet and Grab Bars   130

A Bathroom Vanity   131

10. NEVER SUFFER FROM LACK OF ACCESSIBILITY IN OTHER AREAS IN THE HOME AGAIN   136

11. DOES YOUR CURRENT LAUNDRY ROOM LAYOUT STINK? HERE IS WHAT TO DO   141

Laundry Cabinets   146

PART IV

**HELPFUL ELEMENTS TO HELP YOU
AGE IN PLACE**

12. WHAT IS HOME AUTOMATION AND HOW
DOES IT WORK?   159
13. THE ULTIMATE GUIDE FOR FINDING
PROFESSIONAL HELP AS YOU AGE IN
PLACE   168
14. WHAT EVERYONE MUST KNOW ABOUT
THE FINANCIAL ASSISTANCE AVAILABLE
FOR ACCESSIBLE HOME MODIFICATIONS   176

Conclusion: 193

PART V

MY OTHER BOOKS

Designing Your Forever Home: 198
Human After All   199
Human After All   201

References   203

PART I

INTRODUCTION

This book is about how to create your future accessible home; you never have to leave by incorporating aspects of universal design, aging in place, and accessible design. Accessible design is written in broad terms. I purposely didn't want to write about designing homes for people with specific disabilities because that is not what this book is about. This book is about helping you create an accessible home to help you remain safe and independent through-out your life.

This book is made up of five parts. The first part discusses who would want to 'Age In Place' and why you should take my advice. The second is about Universal Design and Aging

In Place and how they are connected to home design. The third part discusses how to design specific areas around and in your home so you will never have to move. The fourth part of this book states the different types of professionals, services, and resources available to you. The fourth part of this book also discusses the additional funding resources available to you. In this book's fifth and final part, I showcase the other two books I wrote that are available for purchase.

WHO WANTS TO AGE IN PLACE? WHY TAKE MY ADVICE?

If you are lucky enough to grow older, you will want to live in a house where you can access every room as independently as possible.

As you read this book, I want you to consider the following questions: Do you have trouble getting around your house? Are you currently recovering from a total hip or knee replacement? Do you use a cane or walker to help you get around? Do you want to invite your aging parents for Christmas but can not because you have steep stairs in your home?

Have you ever wished you could have a house on one level? Have you ever needed or wanted a bedroom or bathroom on the first floor of your home?

Have you ever wanted to build your dream house and live in it for the rest of your life?

If you answered those questions with a yes, keep reading this book to learn ways to design your home to be accessible for you and your visitors.

If you knew how useful it was to make your home accessible, you would have done it years ago.

I want to discuss how to design an accessible home for you, your family, and your visitors using Universal Design and Aging in Place. You will learn about the benefits of having an accessible home in the first chapter.

Universal design is the design of an environment, building, object, or idea EVERYONE can use (or access) with ease and comfort. You will learn more about universal design in the second chapter.

Aging in Place is the ability to live in your home as long as you like while getting any assistance you require as your needs change regardless of age or ability. .(AgeInPlace.com, 2019) You will learn more about Aging in Place in the third chapter.

In the rest of this book, you will learn about how to best age in place in the different areas of your house, the various people, and the many programs that are available (in the USA) that can help you maintain your independence.

Let me start with a brief family history of me, my family, and my 'journey' with design. My name is Kate Bigalk. I grew up on a farm outside Harmony, MN, with my sister and brother. Most aspects of my childhood were typical (school, homework, family vacations). Other parts of my childhood were challenging, like having a physical disability and using a wheelchair. My childhood experiences fueled my desire to look at the design of homes from a different perspective.

When I was younger, my father and his friends installed an elevator in the house I grew up in, so I could access my bedroom and the upstairs bathroom. Throughout the years, my dad also made a more oversized main bathroom downstairs. He installed "lever door handles" on the doors and an indoor ramp over the back stairs so it would be easier for me to access the house on my own. My dad and his friends also built a deck with custom seating (doubled as a railing), a porch swing, and a custom ramp from the back.

I realized that the same design choices my family put into our house to make it accessible for me also helped other people. For instance, with the ramps we had in our house, everyone could access the main areas of our home. The door handles were 'usable' for everyone. Everyone loved the oversized bathroom downstairs. The seating on our deck provided seating and safety and looked good.

I learned early on that if you design something, you must make it look good and be 'usable' for EVERYONE.

Fast forward to the summer of my junior year of high school (1996), I was working with the librarian at the public library in Harmony, MN. The librarian served on the city council and told me that the library would move and the current building would become the visitor center. The board needed to update the bathrooms to make them more accessible to the public. The librarian asked me for advice on making one bathroom and the overall building more accessible to the public. I offered my suggestions to her. She presented my recommendations to the city board, and the city board approved my requests and made the changes to the building's bathroom.

Today the current visitor center is more 'accessible' to everyone, people in wheelchairs or scooters or people with service animals, to use comfortably. The bathroom is also big enough for parents with children in strollers, bikers, or anyone who needs more help or privacy. My input and advice from the harmony city council provided the community with the opportunity for everyone to have better access to community information and the ability to safely and comfortably use a public bathroom.

You may think, Kate, that is good for you, but what does that have to do with designing an accessible house?

In 2000, our mom and I designed her new one-level home with a basement. That home incorporated elements of Universal Design to help my mother Age in Place. That home had a three-stall garage, two bedrooms, two baths, one-half bath, a laundry room, an office, a kitchen/dining area, and a living room, all on one level. That house had a finished basement with two bedrooms, a bathroom, a kitchenette, a utility room, and storage space. Our mom wanted a space where my sister, brother, and their future families would have a place to stay when visiting.

In 2006 I designed a wheelchair-accessible home for myself. That home had two bedrooms, two baths, a 1 1/2 car garage, a fully accessible kitchen, a dining space, an office, and a living room. I also helped the cabinet maker design a custom 'toe kick' for me to get my toes under the cabinets while seated in a wheelchair.

In 2015 I moved down South and helped my brother-in-law design a wheelchair-accessible "tiny" home. It was around 520 square feet. The tiny house had three 'rooms' one "big" room with a bed, a countertop (for eating and a place for the microwave), a one-well sink, a small refrigerator, cabinets for storage, and a roll-under counter to put my computer on. The second 'room' was a fully accessible bathroom. The third room was a closet with a stacked washer/dryer unit.

In the fall of 2021, after some life changes and the new desire to downsize her 20-some-year house and yard work, my mom, my sister, my brother-in-law, and I helped our mom design her new house. Mom no longer wanted a basement but desired living space over the garage for guests. She wanted less square footage overall, an 'open concept,' AND needed a sunny room facing the South to read in. Mom wanted to upgrade the house she was used to, so she chose a 'Modern Farmhouse' Style house.

Mom incorporated some universal design principles into the design of her new house. For instance, her new home is on a slab the sidewalk wraps around to the cement patio. No steps are going into the house, the garage, or the patio. The landscaping from the sidewalk and patio gradually slopes toward the street.

The people who have visited her home have commented on how much they love the house's open concept. They love the shiplap accents, the windows, the barn doors, the fixtures, and the accessibility features.

Mom said, "From the first night, I have felt at home in this house."

Our friend has told me there is "Not a thing I would do to change it."

That is all a daughter could hope for: to make a mother happy and safe in their "forever" home.

On September 26, 2022, Mary Whalen from the Fillmore County Journal wrote an article about my involvement in designing my mother's house incorporating Aging in Place.

The homes I have helped design have always included the concepts of Universal Design, 'Aging in Place,' style, and function. (Whalen, 2022)

Designing a home is an incredibly daunting task. There are so many questions to think about creating a home. Do I need to remodel my house, or do I need to build a new home? If so, how much will it cost? What do I need or want in my home? Who can help me?

Designing or remodeling a home becomes even more daunting when you add a disability or an extra challenge.

I want to help you design your accessible home because what you're about to learn allowed me to create many accessible homes and spaces in my past.

After discussing my experience designing homes that incorporate wheelchair-accessible and Age-in-Place features, I want to help you create your accessible home.

Before I tell you about aging in place and how you can make your house more accessible. First, I need to tell you about the benefits of having an accessible home.

2

———

THE REASON WHY YOU REALLY NEED AN ACCESSIBLE HOME

Before discussing the benefit of having an accessible home, I would like to share some general knowledge.

First, there is a 60% probability that any new house (over its lifespan) in the United States of America will have a resident with a physical disability. The issue of home accessibility affects older people, people with disabilities, family members, caregivers, and visitors. The importance of designing and building an accessible home will likely grow due to the increasingly aging population. (MacLachlan et al., 2018)

Most older adults wish to continue living independently in their own homes in the communities of their preference. Many older adults with illnesses and other ailments face living in houses that are no longer accessible. These illnesses and conditions threaten safety, quality of life, and where they live. Due to inaccessible homes and communities, many have to move into expensive nursing homes or other settings. These different living arrangements diminish people's quality of life and are costly for the residents and society. (MacLachlan et al., 2018)

What about the availability of accessible homes for people with disabilities? There is little doubt that having an accessible home can enable people with disabilities to live independently. An inaccessible home may cause people with disabilities or other impairments to fall and get injured. An inaccessible home will also restrict the social life of the person with a disability, increasing the hardship on caregivers and the access to social services. The person may be stuck indoors or in one area of the home due to a lack of accessibility, which violates human rights and diminishes the quality of life. (MacLachlan et al., 2018)

A Look at Accessibility

Let us look at the benefits of an accessible home.

The accessible home allows many people to enter, move, and exit homes as independently as possible. An accessible home is best built using universal design or achieved through home modifications. (MacLachlan et al., 2018)

Why should you care about having an accessible environment or house? What are the benefits? Accessibility is not just about having access to a specific environment; it is about understanding why accessible spaces benefit everyone and how to create inclusive spaces. (Heimerdinger, 2021)

Accessible Environments: Physical and Cognitive Barriers

Accessible environments consider the needs and abilities of the people accessing the space. Solutions to physical barriers faced by people with physical disabilities include installing a ramp and a power-operated (either by button or motion-activated) door. An accessible environment can benefit everyone. Almost everyone can benefit from using a ramp or other alternatives to ensure independence in that environment. (Heimerdinger, 2021)

An inclusive environment that can be accessed independently by most people benefits the person in that specific environment; incorporating accessible design can also help places of business, worship centers, individual homes, and society.

Before learning how to make a home as accessible as possible for current and future needs, let us talk about the RESALE value of an accessible home.

The Resale Value of an Accessible Home

Homes built using Universal Design principles make the house accessible for those who live in the house to help boost resale value. What is the resale value of an accessible home? (Fregenal 2019)

Fregenal (2019) stated that the following modifications would help the home's resale value.

- Install a ramp or have a no-step entrance to make it easier for a person using a walker or wheelchair to enter the home.
- Ensure that all interior and exterior doors and doorways are at least 36 inches wide.
- Install a walk-in tub in the bathroom(s)
- Install a roll-in shower in the bathroom (s)
- Add grab bars near toilets and showers to provide extra safety.
- Replace doorknobs and faucet handles with lever handles.
- Lower light switches and raise floor outlets so people in wheelchairs can reach them.

What happens at resale?

Life situations change, and homeowners who modify their property for accessibility may need to sell it at some point. The resale value depends on several factors. (Fregenal 2019)

If the home is in a community whose population includes a high number of seniors or disabled people, accessibility modifications will increase a home's resale value. Such features are also appealing to the 35-to-55 age group. Many improvements, such as levered door handles, faucet handles, and wider doorways, appeal to buyers of any age or situation. (Fregenal 2019)

Accessible modifications, and the cost of reversing them, play a role in the resale value of an accessible home. Some changes that may be cheaper to reverse include raising light switches and removing grab bars. Some changes will be more expensive to make, like raising lovered countertops, stovetops, and sinks that accommodate the person who uses a wheelchair. (Fregenal 2019)

Real Estate Agent

A real estate agent who knows their clients' neighborhoods and the value of accessibility modifications can help with the home's marketing and pricing. The agent will present the home to potential buyers who are in the market for accessible home accommodations and know how to negotiate with a buyer who does not need them. (Fregenal 2019)

Why Build an Accessible Home?

Let us review the reason for wanting to build an accessible home. Perhaps hip, knee, or back problems, using a cane or a walker, and having trouble getting around the current house.

Part of a multi-generational home with parents and adult children living together? A family member may live with a new physical, cognitive or other impairment and now need a home that is more accessible to current needs.

No matter the reasons for having an accessible home. This book will teach what to include when designing, remodeling, or building an accessible house.

This chapter showcased the many benefits of having an accessible home.

To talk about aging in place and how to make each area in and around a home more accessible, I will first discuss what everyone should know about universal design as it relates to private home design.

PART II

UNIVERSAL DESIGN AND AGING IN PLACE

3

WHAT EVERYONE OUGHT TO KNOW ABOUT UNIVERSAL DESIGN

Imagine a home everyone could access regardless of age or ability, or anyone could use a patio door independently. Older parents can use a shower without the fear of slipping and falling. A sibling who is color-blind can quickly spot house numbers when driving down the road. This desire for accessibility is behind the universal design movement. (Truehold, 2022)

A universally designed home is free of barriers throughout the house, leading to greater independence. Incorporating universal design from the starting point of building a home, or deciding to remodel a home, has become more common as baby boomers have aged. (Fregenal, 2021)

Universal design is an awareness of consumer products and environments and how to adapt them for usability regardless of ability. Universal design is a progressive way of thinking to anticipate future needs. (Fregenal, 2021)

The History of Universal Design

Universal design is essential to keep in mind when aging in place. New homes will likely be built or modified using universal design, especially when prospective residents have functional limitations. (Aging In Place, 2022b)

The principles of universal design were in the work of author Selwyn Goldsmith, the author of the book *Designing for the Disabled,* a pioneering book on barrier-free concepts, in 1963. Drawing on Selwyn's work, Architect Ronald L. Mace coined the term "universal design" in 1985 to describe environments usable for everyone, regardless of age or physical ability. (Aging In Place, 2022c)

The development of modern medicine (leading to the increase in life expectancy) has encouraged universal design in homebuilding. (Aging In Place, 2022c)

Universal design is closely related to inclusive design and includes making buildings and products more usable for everyone. (Aging In Place, 2022c)

Universal Design and Accessibility

One of the central principles of universal design is the accessibility movement, which began in the 1960s. Accessibility became a significant factor in home design during the early 1980s. The development of various assistive technologies allowed architects to blend accessibility with style. (Aging In Place, 2022c)

Accessibility looks at the design of a product, service, or environment most usable for people with disabilities. The two ways to look at accessibility; are direct and indirect. (Aging In Place, 2022c)

Direct accessibility allows the person to access/use an object, for example, using a ramp without assistance. (Aging In Place, 2022c)

Indirect accessibility means the user's assistive technology will help access the environment. An example is an automatic door (an app or a button on the wall). (Aging In Place, 2022c)

According to Everstead (2020), everyone should be able to visit your house regardless of age or ability. A great example of this is a house with a no-step front entrance to help people in wheelchairs, those with walkers, parents pushing strollers, oversized luggage, and furniture, or someone with an armful of grocery sacks access the home more accessible. (Everstead, 2020).

Another example has the home's light switches 36 inches off the ground and electrical outlets 18 inches off the floor, more accessible for people to reach. (Everstead, 2020)

A third example of having a home that everyone can visit is to have a roll-in shower in one main-level bathroom, with a portable or flip-up seat and easy-to-reach controls, making it easier for anyone to use. (Everstead, 2020)

Universal Home Design is For Everyone

Universal design is for everyone. Anyone can choose to bring universal design features into their home. A focus on aging in place anticipates common challenges older adults face. If the goal is to retire in own house, universal design can help make that possible. (Everstead, 2020)

What is Universal Design in Housing?

Universal design in housing strives for inclusivity and to create respectful and considerate spaces for people of all ages, abilities, and backgrounds. The creators of universal design intend to accommodate the needs of others who live in or visit home. Architects, engineers, and product designers customize a home to suit unique requirements. (Truehold, 2022)

The 8 Goals of Universal Home Design

Truhold (2022) states the eight main goals of universal design according to The University of Buffalo.

1. **Body fit:** The home is suitable for various body sizes and abilities.
2. **Comfort:** A home and its amenities are within reasonable and desirable limits of body function and perception.

3. **Awareness:** Critical information is easy to perceive by others in the home.
4. **Understanding:** Home amenities' are straightforward and intuitive.
5. **Wellness:** The home is safe and healthy for all users.
6. **Social integration:** Home's design treats users with dignity and respect.
7. **Personalization:** home design incorporates needs while emphasizing the ability to express individual preferences.
8. **Cultural appropriateness:** The home respects cultural values

Confused as to what the above goals are referring to? So was I. So I wanted to find some real-life examples of universal design. Below are seven real-life examples of Universal Design:

Seven Real-Life Examples of Universal Design

In the late 1990s, Architects, Product Designers, Engineers, and Environmental Design researchers from North Carolina State University created seven principles of Universal Design. These principles serve as the design of home environments and products, but they are not a rulebook. Instead, they can apply these principles for the overall benefit of any person. (Truehold, 2022)

Principle 1: Equitable Use.

The design is helpful to people from all walks of life and abilities.

Real-life example: A roll-in shower with visual contrast and increased friction will help people of all abilities. The shower with a handheld showerhead, grab bars, and other accessibility-focused amenities. (Truehold, 2022)

Principle 2: Flexibility in Use.

The home's design accommodates a wide range of individual preferences and abilities.

Real-life example: A multi-level countertop and open shelving kitchen island accommodate personal preferences and abilities. (Truehold, 2022)

Principle 3: Simple & Intuitive Use.

A home's appliances and fixtures are easy to understand and operate, regardless of users' experience, language skills, or capacity for concentration.

Real-life example: The home has a digital thermostat. This type of thermostat mimics the old thermostat with dials. The thermostat design is easy to understand regardless of the user's experience, knowledge, or language skills. (Truehold, 2022)

Principle 4: Perceptible Information.

The home communicates all necessary information to the people, regardless of sensory capabilities or lighting conditions. (Truehold, 2022)

Real-life example: big, bold address numbers communicate their meaning effectively to the user. (Truehold, 2022)

Principle 5: Tolerance for Error.

The design of the home anticipates possible accidents and hazards.

Real-life example: A kitchen with an induction-type stovetop that only heats up when metal pots or pans are on it. (Truehold, 2022)

Principle 6: Low Physical Effort.

The home's design minimizes fatigue.

Real-life example: A home plan is intuitive, one-level, and free of barriers (Truehold, 2022)

Principle 7: Size & Space for Approach & Use.

The home is highly usable, despite body size, height, or mobility.

Real-life example: Wide hallways and open floor plans are throughout the home, making it highly usable. (Truehold, 2022)

Incorporating Universal Design into a Home

There are many reasons to build a home with universal design features, including life-changing accidents, rare illnesses, surgeries, broken bones, visiting relatives, and increased home value. (Everstead, 2020)

Lifestyle and Future

An accidental injury is nearly unavoidable with an active lifestyle or having active children. Independently navigating a house on a broken leg or after surgery can become challenging. A roll-in shower can make a difference when recovering from recent surgery, and wide doorways can relieve walking with crutches. Why not live in a home that can accommodate those events when accidents happen? (Everstead, 2020)

Family and Friends Visiting

Love to entertain or have a friend or relative visit, a simple, inclusive design feature, such as a bathroom or bedroom on the main floor, can make a home visitable for all. After all, no one wants to turn away a loved one from visiting their home because it is not accessible. (Everstead, 2020)

Home Value

A home with a universal design can be more marketable. Universal design can also be a virtual and desirable feature that may not even notice. Intelligent design choices are valuable to buyers and will benefit the seller. (Everstead, 2020)

In this chapter, I write about the definition of Universal Design. I look at a brief history of universal design concerning environments and homes. I write about how universal design and accessibility are intertwined with each other. Finally, I highlight what universal design is and why you should incorporate Universal Design into your home.

The next chapter is about Aging in Place.

4

OK, SO. HOW DO I AGE IN PLACE?

S uppose your overall "end" goal is to stay in the home as long as possible. This idea, essentially, is what 'Aging-In-Place' is all about. The idea is to build a home so that everyday tasks require the least amount of physical effort. It is essential to cover all anticipated long-term needs to stay in the house as long as possible. It is much easier to build for the future now. Home modifications will be much more disruptive later. (HOMEBUILDING / REMODELING GUIDE, 2022)

To achieve greater accessibility at home and live as independently as possible, the house will have to be remodeled. (Fregenal, 2021)

You may be thinking, "Ok, So. How Do I AGE IN PLACE?" In this short chapter, you will be BRIEFLY learning how to design your home, who can help you, and what an Aging-In-Place renovation entails.

Please take the following advice from the HOMEBUILDING / REMODELING GUIDE (2022) to heart.

Six Aging-In-Place Design Recommendations

#1 – Build A Single-Story House

A single-story house ensures that everything will be accessible throughout the home's interior, regardless of aging or mobility issues. (HOMEBUILDING/REMODELING GUIDE, 2022)

#2 – A Smaller House May Be Better

When deciding the size of a new home, ask yourself this question: "how much house will you want to clean?" The answer must be a house that is manageable, easy to clean, and accommodates you. (HOMEBUILDING/REMODELING GUIDE, 2022)

#3 – Flooring Considerations

A floor must be safe, convenient, and stylish! HOMEBUILDING/REMODELING GUIDE (2022) recommends installing a non-slippery floor. Some examples of non-slippery flooring are cork, bamboo, and vinyl.

#4 – Kitchen Universal Design Features

A kitchen should have plenty of space, good lighting, and many accessible features. To make the kitchen a functional space for all ages and abilities, choose multi-level counter-tops in the kitchen. Cabinet hardware should also be easy to grasp and pulls instead of knobs. Pulls allow anyone with dexterity issues to use their whole hand instead of just their fingertips. (HOMEBUILDING / REMODELING GUIDE, 2022)

#5 – Bathroom Universal Design Features

A traditional interior door will swing in against a wheelchair inside. Consider using a 36-inch wide pocket or barn door (instead of a conventional swing door) as an entrance to the main bathroom. Have at least five feet of open space to allow a wheelchair (in case one is needed) to turn around in the bathroom. A 'roll under' bathroom vanity is helpful for anyone in a wheelchair to get closer to the sink. A higher toilet, at least 16" to 17", requires less bending down, making it more accessible than a shorter one. The ensuite bathroom must be big enough to have a roll-in shower and bathtub (if needed). Getting in and out of a tub can be more challenging for older adults. (HOMEBUILDING / REMODELING GUIDE, 2022)

#6 – Master Bedroom Universal Design Features

Size and space are essential considerations in the main bedroom. A large bedroom will be beneficial for a wheelchair in the future. (HOMEBUILDING / REMODELING GUIDE, 2022)

A nother factor to consider as you 'age in place is the home's exterior maintenance.

Elements of A Maintenance-Free Home

Low-maintenance features and must-haves for a home include windows, siding, gutters, and a deck. (HOME-BUILDING/REMODELING GUIDE, 2022)

1. **Windows** — Choose vinyl or wood windows with vinyl or aluminum on the exterior.
2. **Siding** — Brick and vinyl siding products only require occasional cleaning. The brick will last the home's life, and many vinyl siding products have a 20-year-plus warranty. **Gutters** — a gutter blocks debris from entering and directs water away from the house.
3. **Deck** — install a deck made of composite decking material instead of a traditional wood deck. A standard deck requires yearly maintenance and costs a lot to maintain its beauty. Composite materials will last 20 or more years and require very

little or no maintenance to keep them looking beautiful.

The next question will have, "Who can help me?" There is one specialist who can help; they are known as a Certified Aging-in-Place Specialist (CAPS).

What is a Certified Aging-in-Place Specialist (CAPS)?

Certified Aging-in-Place Specialist trains in the needs, tools, and regulations regarding universal home design: once certified, a CAPS professional must complete continuing education each year. The demand for such professionals is increasing because many baby boomers live longer and want (and are offered) different housing options than their parent's generation. (Fregenal, 2021)

What Does an Aging-in-Place Specialist Do?

· · ·

CAPS professionals are usually remodelers, general contractors, designers, architects, or healthcare professionals. A CAPS helps homeowners make modifications that create a safe and comfortable home to help homeowners live independently. The specialist can install grab bars next to toilets and tubs and in showers, replace doorknobs with lever handles, and install handrails on stairways. A CAPS can make doors and doorways wider, install a ramp, a low-maintenance yard, lower appliances or cabinetry, and pull-down shelves. (Walker, 2022)

The National Association of Home Builders (NAHB) lists current CAPS-certified contractors and professionals. (Fregenal, 2021)

What Does a CAPS Aging-In-Place Renovation Mean?

The object of remodeling a current home or building a new home (to age-in-place in) is to minimize injury and accidents. Some renovations include installing bathroom grab bars and lever-style door handle instead of round doorknobs. Other options are to lower kitchen appliances to countertop height and to change light switches to toggle or rocker-type switches. More extensive renovations include widening doorways and hallways and making entryways level. For new homes, stacking closets on top of each other allows installing an elevator later, if necessary. (Fregenal, 2021)

Keep in mind; that it is easier to build for the future now — Home modifications will be much more disruptive later. (HOMEBUILDING / REMODELING GUIDE, 2022)

In this chapter, I write about the definition of Aging-in-Place. I briefly highlight six aging-in-place design recommendations. I write about a specific type of professional you want to work with when designing and building your home. Finally, I write about what an aging-In-place renovation entails.

You may feel overwhelmed by where to start your home modification and what to do first. I recommend starting at the main entrance of your home. The next part of this book discusses what you need to know about making the exterior and interior of your home more accessible for you to age in place.

PART III

AGING IN PLACE: AROUND YOUR HOME

The following seven chapters take a more in-depth look at different aspects of aging in place around the home.

5

WHAT YOU NEED TO KNOW ABOUT AN ACCESSIBLE HOME EXTERIOR AND ENTRANCE

A home's entryway is crucial because it provides access to the house. A home's entrance often includes steps, presenting a safety challenge for some people. Some entryway modifications take time and are expensive, like installing a ramp or nonskid flooring. Other measures need slight changes to the home, such as installing new light switches and railings. Many modifications are as inexpensive as removing throw rugs and adding new light fixtures. (Aging In Place, 2022c)

Modifying Entryways for Accessibility

One common remodel modification done first to a home is changing at least one entrance so that it is completely covered and has no steps to get inside. Another improvement is replacing or installing lever door handles to avoid difficulty opening a door. (Aging In Place, 2022c)

One must ensure that a home's entrances have enough lighting to see.

Lighting Modifications At Home Entry Points

The most crucial lighting modification is to increase the light surrounding the entryway. Exterior lighting at a home's entrance is critical since steps, doorknobs, and door locks must be seen and used efficiently. Having multiple external light sources is necessary, so someone inside can see visitors' faces and homeowners can see the house's distinguishing features, like house numbers. Backlighting is also an effective method of seeing house numbers, day or night. (Aging In Place, 2022c)

Security

Home security and protection from criminals or any other threats is the foundation of any safety plan for the home. An exterior motion section light is a great way to alert to the presence of someone outside the home. These entry lights are activated when they detect motion above a certain threshold and turn off automatically after a specified period of inactivity. (Aging In Place, 2022c)

. . .

Entry Points

The entryway to a home provides ways to improve safety and security for seniors. Safety and security measures include improvements made to doors, windows, and locks. Electronic peepholes are also an effective method of increasing an entry point's security. These safety and security measures can reduce the probability of an incident occurring and minimize harm if an incident does occur. (Aging In Place, 2022c)

An extra safety and security measure is ensuring that all exterior doors and frames are metal or solid wood. The doors should have deadbolts and be locked at all times, regardless of the neighborhood's safety. (Aging In Place, 2022c)

Exterior doors with full-length glass windows may look great but are unsafe. The glass makes the inside of a home evident to anyone outside, even if the glass is frosted. As an extra safety measure, replace any exterior door that contains glass. A spare house key should never be in a prominent location. Only trusted friends and family should have a copy of the house keys. (Aging In Place, 2022c)

As for windows, replace the glass with safety glass. This glass is virtually unbreakable. The safety glass will make it hard to force entry through the windows and increase the window's structural strength. Even though it is thicker than standard glass, it will still be transparent. Still concerned about safety, install a security film on the interior side of the glass to prevent it from shattering. (Aging In Place, 2022c)

Peephole

A 'traditional' peephole on an exterior door is a traditional method of identifying the person on the other side. Interior lighting is critical for maximizing the effectiveness of a peephole. The height of the peephole should be enough to look out conveniently and see the person's face. (Aging In Place, 2022c)

On the other hand, an electronic peephole provides an accurate image of the person outside the door. Electronic peepholes use batteries and an LCD panel to display a larger image. The LCD panel offers a zoom display mode, can compensate for low-light conditions, and prevents interior light from exiting the peephole. The doorbell may need to be lowered from its standard location for it to be accessed by most people. (Aging In Place, 2022c)

Entrance Shelves or Seats

Many people tend to unlock and push the door open in two short moves; doing so with boxes in hand might cause falling accidents if an entrance has a step. A shelf or seat by the door is handy because it can provide a place to set packages while finding keys and opening the door and will help prevent falls at the main entry in the future. (Age In Place, 2022b)

Sidewalk and Steps

The sidewalk should be 36 inches wide and not steep. If the sidewalk is prone to be slippery or uneven in places, consider having a textured surface applied to it; so it will not become a tripping hazard. (Age In Place, 2022b)

Another suggestion from Age In Place (2022b) is to keep shrubs, bushes, and trees cut back on both sides of your sidewalks and steps and to install path lighting.

The steps leading to the home's entrance must have a textured surface and handrails on both sides of the steps to prevent falls. If the home has multiple steps, consider leaving enough space around the house for a future ramp in the future. Alternatively, removing steps, and adding a ramp, reduce the risk of falling and makes it easier for everyone to get outside and inside a home. (Age In Place, 2022b)

Exterior Maintenance

There are four areas to be aware of when preparing outside the home. Low-maintenance exterior construction, roof and downspouts, low-maintenance landscaping, and ramps. (Age In Place, 2022b)

1. Low-Maintenance Exterior Construction

First, low-maintenance exterior construction outside the home will ensure minimal upkeep. (Age In Place, 2022b)

2. Roof and Downspouts

The roof is a home's first defense system, and the type of material used to construct it makes a big difference. Various roofing materials impact a home's look, function, and longevity. The two common roof materials are metal and shingles. Both styles have their advantages and disadvantages to consider. (Advocate Construction, 2022)

A. Roof Materials

- **Metal Roof**

Pros of Metal Roofing

According to Advocate Construction (2022), a metal roof has some advantages.

- A metal roof is low maintenance, allows a traditional look or an option to get creative, and can last a lifetime, positively affecting property value. A metal roof has longevity, so buyers do not have to worry about additional upfront roofing costs. (Advocate Construction, 2022)

- Metal roofs are eco-friendly, use recycled materials, are recyclable, and reduce energy use. Refracted heat from home can appeal to a future buyer who cares about cost and the environment. Even solar panels are easier to install on metal roofs. (Advocate Construction, 2022)

- Metal is the most robust material to build a roof and provides a substantial barrier against the elements. They are designed to withstand damage, will not need repairing after a heavy storm, and is fire-resistant. The most important pro of a metal roof is that it has a longer lifespan, sometimes lasting 50-100 years. (Advocate Construction, 2022)

Cons of Metal Roofing

According to Advocate Construction (2022), a metal roof has some disadvantages.

- Metal roofing is more labor intensive
- Requires a skilled professional to install.
- There are not as many roofers with the experience to install as shingle roofers.

Homeowners Associations

Homeowners Associations can have strict rules and regulations for their residents. Metal is newer to the industry's residential roofing side so some municipalities may ban them. Before starting any home project, it is essential to check with the Homeowners Association. (Advocate Construction, 2022)

Insurance Problems

Sometimes, metal roofs will give insurance benefits. Other times, there may be problems. Since metal roofs are expensive, insurance companies could increase premiums in case of replacement. (Advocate Construction, 2022)

B. Shingle Roof

An asphalt shingle roof is a more common type in residential areas. It is often the "traditional" roof used for most homes.

According to Advocate Construction (2022), an asphalt shingle roof is the most "traditional" type used for most homes. The following are some advantages of a shingle roof to consider.

Advantages of A Shingle Roof

- **Practical**

A shingle roof is cheaper to install, more economical, and quicker to fix due to the lower material cost. Walking on a shingle roof is possible, so cleaning and maintaining it is more manageable. (Advocate Construction, 2022)

- **Easy to Install**

Shingles are easier to transport and also offer a more straightforward, quicker installation process. Many contractors have experience with shingles, so finding a qualified professional is quick. There is some excellent warranty coverage on the market. The manufacturer and the contractor may provide a warranty option for shingle roofs. (Advocate Construction, 2022)

. . .

Cons of Shingle Roofing

- A Shingle roof has a shorter life cycle, rarely lasting longer than 25 years. They succumb to flaking and are breeding grounds for algae, mold, and mildew. Shingle roofs usually need some shingles replaced or repaired before a total roof replacement. (Advocate Construction, 2022)

- Shingle roofs do not have the array of style and color options that metal roofing offers. It is tough to dye a shingle or find one light in color. The asphalt limits the opportunity for vivid colors on shingle roofs. Shingles will fade over time and get darker in the sun. (Advocate Construction, 2022)

- Shingle roofs absorb heat because of the color and chemical makeup of the asphalt. The transferred heat can cause a spike in utilities. Additionally, asphalt can burn quickly, which can be detrimental in the case of house fires. (Advocate Construction, 2022)

- Shingles are made from an oil-based product, making them difficult to recycle. While it is possible, most people are unaware of how to dispose of shingles properly, so they end up in landfills. (Advocate Construction, 2022)

Cost of Metal Roof vs. Shingle Roof

When considering the cost of a roof, it is essential to consider both short-term and long-term costs. For instance, while metal roofs are more money upfront, they last longer and are less likely to need repairs over time, costing less. (Advocate Construction, 2022)

- **Rain Gutters**

Rain gutters do more than keep downpours from drenching people as they come and go. They channel water out and away from the home's foundation, reducing the risk of a flooded basement or damaged siding and minimizing erosion and harm to landscaping. (Ullman, 2021)

. . .

S ometimes a house does not need rain gutters, but most do. To figure out if a home needs rain gutters, Ullman (2021) says to consider the following:

- Suppose the roof has no overhang or only has a few inches of overhang. In that case, water will accumulate against the foundation, damage flower beds near it, and pour down on people as they enter or exit the home. *In this scenario, gutters are a must.* (Ullman, 2021)

- If a roof is sharply peaked, rainwater will run away from the house rather than straight down to the ground. *In this case, installing gutters may not be necessary.* (Ullman, 2021)

- If a house is higher than the surrounding landscaping, water is unlikely to "pool" around the foundation of a home, *making gutters optional.* (Ullman, 2021)

- However, if the house is slightly lower than the surrounding ground, *gutters must provide a channel, so the water runoff is a sufficient distance from the foundation.* (Ullman, 2021)

- Suppose concrete on patios, walkways, or driveways surrounds a house. In that case, *rain gutters might be optional,* as the concrete serves as a protective layer between the runoff and the foundation. (Ullman, 2021)

- Rain gutters may not be necessary if a home is in an arid climate. Ullman, 2021)

3. Low-Maintenance Landscaping

Third, having low-maintenance landscaping is essential. This decision will reduce the work required for the homeowner and the expense of a decision to use a lawn care company eventually. Consider having landscape and yard accents that do not require care. (Age In Place, 2022b)

. . .

4. Wheelchair Ramps

Many people do not wish to have a ramp installed in front of their homes because they dislike their appearance. However, ramps can complement the home's style and make it easier for everyone to enter a home. (AgingInPlace.org, 2022b)

Planning

- Before installing a wheelchair ramp, the first step is considering its primary users. Look at their assistive devices, which may include canes, crutches, and wheelchairs. Furthermore, it would help to think about future abilities changes before building a ramp. (AgingInPlace.org, 2022b)

- Various regulations can also affect the planning phase for this construction project, including the local municipality's zoning laws and building codes. Check with the local building department to obtain any necessary permits. A homeowners' association (HOA) may impose additional restrictions on wheelchair ramps within your neighborhood, especially if it is visible. Climate and the prevalence of natural disasters also affect design choices. (AgingInPlace.org, 2022b)

- Before building a ramp, think about the best entrance to install the ramp. Consider how much room there is and if physical barriers, such as bushes, trees, and walkways, can also be factors. (AgingInPlace.org, 2022b)

- The ramps' steepness and slope depend on the entry point above ground level and may also be subject to limitations imposed by local building codes. When choosing an entrance to make accessible, consider the entrance's ease of access and doorway widths. Finally, the ramp should accommodate doorway features such as platforms, porches, and stairs. (AgingInPlace.org, 2022b)

Design

. . .

The most critical design considerations for a wheelchair ramp are its slope and length. The ramp's slope is significant as it affects other factors, such as its layout, accessibility, and construction cost. (AgingIn-Place.org, 2022b)

The slope is usually 1:12, meaning the ramp rises one inch for every 12 inches of its run, the most common slope for a wheelchair ramp. Check the local building codes for compliance if planning to deviate from this standard. (AgingIn-Place.org, 2022b)

A wheelchair ramp comprises sloped segments, also known as ramp segments, separated by flat segments and landings. The purpose of the landing is to allow the person pushing the wheelchair to rest. The length of each ramp segment determines its rise, which should never exceed 30 inches. The length of each ramp segment should be no more than 30 feet. Landings should be five feet long and five feet wide, with enough space to allow a change in direction. (AgingIn-Place.org, 2022b)

Handrails

Handrails should be on both sides of a ramp, be between 34 and 38 inches high, and 1 1/2 inches deep between the rail and any solid surface outside the ramp. (AgingInPlace.org, 2022b)

. . .

Materials

The primary physical requirements for the ramp surface are to be firm, stable, and slip-resistant in any weather. One suggestion is to build a ramp with a low-maintenance composite material, so the ramp surface remains maintenance-free. The handrails should also be constructed of composite materials to be low-maintenance and comfortable. (AgingInPlace.org, 2022b)

Construction

Building codes and other considerations make constructing a wheelchair ramp a relatively complex and involved process, so find a contractor specializing in ADA-compliant modifications. (AgingInPlace.org, 2022b)

Wheelchair Ramp Lighting

Wheelchair ramps create a common challenge in providing an entryway with adequate lighting. Low-voltage lights offer an effective solution for lighting a wheelchair ramp. They can be for wheelchair ramps by mounting them to the sides of the ramp, providing continual lighting along the entire ramp length. Deck lights can be mounted, making them flush with the ramp surface, not creating an obstacle for the wheelchair. Considerations for wheelchair ramp lighting underscore the importance of proper lighting in all home areas. Furthermore, deck lights are dimmer than traditional lighting, so they are less likely to blind someone who looks directly at them. (AgingInPlace.org, 2022b)

The Deck

A deck made of composite decking material is durable, requires little upkeep, is environmentally friendly, and can be in various colors and finishes.

Interior Lighting

Light in a home can directly affect the quality of life. Proper lighting in a home can improve vision, independence, and safety by reducing the risk of slips and falls. Lighting is essential because our vision tends to weaken due to regular age-related changes, and eye diseases become more prevalent as a person ages. Our eyes' loss of efficiency in gathering light creates specific vision problems, such as increased sensitivity to light and the time needed to adapt to changes in light level. (AgingInPlace.org, 2022b)

* * *

The Garage

The Location of The Garage

One aspect of a home is having a garage convenient to the home's main level and accessible by anyone. A garage close to the home's entrance will make the trek to and from home more straightforward when hauling packages to and from the car. However, the garage is for more than parking a vehicle. In their garages, people also have freezers, tools, storage, and utilities. (Age In Place, 2022a)

When building a new home, have an attached garage or a short enclosed breezeway connecting to the house. If the garage is far away, make an enclosed breezeway from the garage to the home and build a gradually sloping ramp inside the breezeway (instead of stairs). The ramp will be more accessible for anyone to use now and in the future.

Having an attached garage is a safe and convenient option for anyone, but especially for a person who wants to age in place. The person will be out of the elements, use fewer steps going to and from home, and a vehicle will be much closer.

The following suggestions from Age In Place (2022a) are ideas to help you plan a usable garage space.

Space to Move

A garage will need to be wider than usual to accommodate people in wheelchairs, who use walkers, and their caregivers. So, try to leave five feet between vehicles to get in and out. (Age In Place, 2022a)

Garage Door

Opening an automatic garage door is as simple as pressing a button. The sensors automatically stop the door from closing if something gets in the door. For homeowners, home security is a top priority. Invest in a high-security garage door, especially if the garage is attached to the home. Steel garage doors are secure and prevent most intruders from entering the house. Poor garage door insulation can make it more complex and expensive to keep a home cool. Ensuring the door is insulated correctly provides more control over the garage's temperature and drowns out the outside noises coming from a busy road. (H, 2020)

Upgrading from a car to SUV makes it easier to access the vehicle. Taller vehicles are better for those who use a cane, walker, or wheelchair because they will not strain joints. Ensure the garage has enough ceiling clearance to accommodate taller vehicles. Garage doors that tilt up are problematic as they sit against the ceiling, and when opened, they can reduce garage ceiling clearance. A garage door that "roll" up is better if the garage has a low ceiling because it can be wrapped around a spool above the doorway and take up little ceiling space. (H, 2020)

Types of Garage Door Remotes

The standard garage door remote control has a rectangular shape with rounded edges and a clip to attach to a car's sun visor—the design for ease of use. There are mini remotes usually around half the size and can be easily attached to a keychain, making them easy to carry at all times. (Garage Door Repair Peachtree City, 2022)

Different Number Of Buttons On The Remote

Some garage door remotes have one, two, and three buttons, depending on how many doors need control. Some manufacturers that make electric gate openers and devices for lighting automation make multi-purpose remotes that can control all of these devices simultaneously. The same remote can open a gate or garage door and turn on the lights in the garage using the same three buttons. Providing convenience and security since all three functions are in one remote instead of three different remotes. (Garage Door Repair Peachtree City, 2022)

. . .

Other garage door remotes have rolling code technology. This technology makes the garage door remote change to a different access code every time it opens. Meaning it will be impossible for potential intruders to exploit the code. Many models offer WiFi connectivity, making it possible to use a smartphone as a remote. When selecting a new garage door opener remote, consider specific needs based on the security and convenience of new remote models. (Garage Door Repair Peachtree City, 2022)

Install a garage door opener on the interior wall 40 inches off the garage floor and leave space below to access the opener for the area for a wheelchair or walker later in life.

No Step Entry

Make sure there are no steps leading up to the entrance from the garage. If the garage sits lower than the house, a ramp in the garage to allow easy access to the home. A ramp in the garage ensures access to the house while ensuring health and safety from potential thieves. (Age In Place, 2022a)

. . .

Non-Slip Floor

Please install a great-looking non-slip coating on the garage floor to reduce the chance of slipping and falling. (Age In Place, 2022a)

Access/Side Door

The side access door should be 36 inches wide and have a lever handle allowing people of all abilities to use the door. (Age In Place, 2022a)

Garage Lighting

Proper lighting in the garage is a crucial universal design element and will reduce the chance of tripping and falling. Also, ensure that the lights stay on when the garage door opens long enough to get into the house. (Age In Place, 2022a)

Adjustable Storage Shelves

Adjustable storage systems in the garage are an excellent way to keep things organized and in view. A flexible shelving system allows changes as needs change. Several manufacturers offer designs that are available at home improvement stores. (Age In Place, 2022a)

. . .

In this chapter, I discussed designing a house's exterior and entryway to be safer, more efficient, and more accessible. I wrote about a home's entrances, steps, sidewalks, shelves and seats, maintenance, roof types, shingles, and downspouts, and designing wheelchair-accessible ramps and decks. The chapter also discussed exterior lighting, safety, security, ways to create a garage, the best garage location, space needed to move, storage solutions, garage door openers, flooring, doors, and interior lighting.

The next chapter will discuss ways to make a living room more accessible as you age in place.

6

CRACKING THE ACCESSIBLE LIVING ROOM CODE

Before we chat about making specific areas of your home accessible to all who may use it, I want to mention some general recommendations. When remodeling or building an accessible home, one thing to remember is the height of light switches and outlets, the width of the hallway, doorway, and doors, and the best type of flooring.

As a person who uses a wheelchair, I have found that the best type of light switch is a 'rocker' type. A good height for a light switch is 36 inches off of the floor. A good height for an outlet is 18 inches off of the floor.

Doors and doorways should be 36 inches wide to make it easier for a person who uses a wheelchair or walker can safely go through. A great width for a hallway is anything more than 40 inches wide.

I recommend having the same flooring throughout a home to avoid "transitional" bumps. In my opinion, the best type of flooring is one that is waterproof, easy to clean, and durable.

The LIVING ROOM

There are benefits of aging in place, but even the living room, can present physical hazards for people. An end or coffee table could be in the way; an area rug could catch the leg of a walker or bunch up, creating a tripping hazard, which is a problem. (AgingInPlace.org, 2022d)

There are ways to avoid these problems, now is the time to make changes instead of later. In the future, worries about how to make the living room livable, safe, and secure will be non-existent. (AgingInPlace.org, 2022d)

Room to Move Around In The Living Room

Having enough room to get around and accessing everything in a living room is critical when you have personal physical limitations. Having enough space makes a HUGE difference between a comfortable living room and one to avoid. A disability may cause one to struggle with getting from one room to another, going through the living room to use the bathroom, entering the kitchen, or even answering the front door. In short, the living room needs to be big enough. (AgingInPlace.org, 2022d)

Of course, the problem is not always the amount of space. Sometimes, there are too many 'things' in the room. Getting rid of all of your things is an unrealistic goal; after all, the living room is the place to display objects that have sentimental value. Rearranging things is not the same as getting rid of them. Freeing up some much-needed space by moving items to other rooms or giving them to friends and family members will make the area feel less cluttered. (AgingInPlace.org, 2022d)

Ideally, everyone with mobility issues should be able to move about freely in a living room. A person who uses a cane, crutches, a walker, or even a wheelchair should have adequate space to move around. A five-foot turning radius is ideal for a person in a wheelchair to turn around properly. Aging in place addressing such issues since things can change quickly as a person ages. It is better to clear space and have it already open. (AgingInPlace.org, 2022d)

The Layout Matters

When aging in place, consider the size of the living room and having enough uncluttered space; the layout of that space also affects whether one can get around safely. (AgingInPlace.org, 2022d)

All kinds of problems can occur from a bad living room layout. For example, a coffee table with legs that curve outward can trip a person. A wanted object on an end table far from the couch can mean a person risking a fall or strain to get it independently. Getting rid of all the furniture will not fix the issue. Keep the layout simple and efficient. (AgingInPlace.org, 2022d)

When setting up a living room to age in place, these are the questions to ask oneself. Is the coffee table in the way of a transfer from a wheelchair to the couch? Does the sofa slide easily on the wood floors? When setting up a living room to age in place, these are the questions to ask oneself. A living room should look nice and be comfortable and safe. (Aging-InPlace.org, 2022d)

Many people worry they will need to take almost everything out of the living room to have space and forget that they also have to live there. If other people live together or have many visitors, ensure there are comfortable places to sit. Try different layouts to get the best one because not all are equal. The living room layout is essential to ensure the space is safer and easier to navigate. (AgingInPlace.org, 2022d)

Televisions

The size of a TV matters too. A large TV can provide a sharper, clearer screen for someone who enjoys watching TV and wants to see their favorite programs without feeling left out. Closed captioning can also help those who are hard of hearing. (AgingInPlace.org, 2022d)

TV Remotes

Several remotes for different electronics make life difficult. A remote with 70 buttons may not always work. Buy a remote that has large simple buttons. Having fewer things to press makes it harder to make a mistake. Think about how much the TV is being watched and focus on a remote; electronics give those options. Remember that technology changes fast, and new remote-control technologies may emerge (voice commands, for example). (AgingInPlace.org, 2022d)

Look at universal remotes available and find a balance between a design with larger buttons and the functionality for what is needed. A remote that does all the basics can be a good choice for everyday use. Keep the complicated remotes stored away until they are required. (AgingInPlace.org, 2022d)

Anchoring TVs

A TV stand or entertainment center should support the size and weight of the TV. The TV should be anchored on a sturdy, low base and pushed back as far as possible. Use products specifically designed for television anchoring.

(ChildProofingExperts.com & The International Association for Child Safety, 2020)

Televisions are not required to come with anchors, but flat-screen anchoring products are available. A popular safety option is to secure an appropriate wall mount to the wall stud with the proper length screw.

(ChildProofingExperts.com & The International Association for Child Safety, 2020)

So, What About the Other Living Room Furniture?

The home's layout and furniture matter; that old favorite recliner and couch may be comfortable, but getting up may get more complex as time passes. No matter what kind of furniture is in the house, aging in place demands a look ahead, but safety has to take priority. (AgingInPlace.org, 2022d)

Power Sofas and Recliners

A lot has changed in furniture function. One of the latest innovations in this field is automatic power functions. Unlike conventional hand-operated or manual recliners, a power recliner does not require force. All that is needed is to touch a button to adjust sitting positions, leg positions, and head and neck positions. Sit and relax in a favorite place and enjoy a favorite hobby. Most of these recliners can even charge a cell phone or tablet. (Bernal, 2022)

Living Room Flooring

Flooring matters when it comes to protecting people as they age in place, and there are two points of view on flooring. (AgingInPlace.org, 2022d)

Carpet

The carpet is softer than a hard surface floor. A carpet is softer if someone does happen to fall. There is less chance of someone obtaining a broken bone or another injury if they fall on the carpet. Although some types of carpet (shaggy) also make a fall more likely. Choose a low-pile carpet if a hard floor (tile, wood, laminate, or vinyl plank) is not for you. (AgingInPlace.org, 2022d)

Choose a carpet (a low pile and a thinner pad). The thin carpet pad will make the carpet firmer, making it easier to navigate a walker or wheelchair and less likely to cause a tripping hazard. While it may not be an issue now, future personal physical changes that occur could easily affect one's movement around the living room. A carpet firmly in place will be much safer in the long run, reducing the chances of getting injured. (AgingInPlace.org, 2022d)

Hard Flooring

Some people believe that hard flooring (tile, wood, laminate, or vinyl plank) is the right choice because it is easy to clean and less of a tripping hazard. Both arguments have merit. The goal is to prevent falls in the first place. A fall on hard flooring may cause an injury but is less of a tripping hazard overall. Additionally, it is easier to keep clean and makes it easy to move a wheelchair or walker across the space. Although, Be aware that hard floors often mean area rugs which can be a problem and a tripping hazard. (AgingIn-Place.org, 2022d)

Getting Help in an Emergency

In an emergency, getting to a phone fast is vital. Of course, getting to a phone in a non-emergency situation is just as important. Keeping a cell phone in a pocket or clipped to a hip is one of the ways to reduce the risk of not having a phone available (in an emergency), but it is not the only option. There are other choices. (AgingInPlace.org, 2022d)

Medical Pendants

A medical alert pendant can reach out to help in an emergency. However, the pendant alerts the monitoring company first, then the appropriate emergency authorities. However, they are not a good choice for minor issues where a neighbor or a family member could come over and provide a little help, not emergency responders; most of the time, access to a phone is all needed. (AgingInPlace.org, 2022d)

Living Room Lighting

One significant risk for older people is not seeing enough to navigate furniture and other obstacles. If the lighting in the living room is poor, a person could trip over something or get hurt in some other way. However, changing the ceiling lights should not be that difficult for the most part and is vital for avoiding accidents. Have a switch near the door to turn on the lights when walking through the room. Have a light switch closer to a favorite reading chair or couch, so there is good lighting when reading. (AgingInPlace.org, 2022d)

Lamps

Additionally, have extra light by using lamps. These lamps must not easily break if knocked over. Hide lamp cords to prevent tripping and have fewer lamps in areas where a person might use a walker or wheelchair. (AgingInPlace.org, 2022d)

Currently, there are many ways to operate a lamp. There is the traditional switch on the wall, the pull chain option, the rotary turn style switch, a push button option (either placed on the floor or table), and a touch lamp option. Plugging a lamp into a unique outlet connected to a home automation network system can operate the lamp hands-free.

The kind of lighting matters, as well. Choose energy-efficient bulbs that mimic daylight, which can help mood and make it easier to see. With these bulbs, the extra lighting will also be easier on the electric bill. This lightbulb lasts a long time. The quality of light is much better than a standard bulb, making it cost-effective and safer in the long run. (AgingInPlace.org, 2022d)

Do You Eat or Sleep In The Living Room?

Many people like to eat in the living room to watch TV. Some people may have health conditions or chronic pain that make sleeping in a recliner easier. Because of that, it is good to plan to be ready when things change. Perhaps placing a tray on a chair armrest will make eating in front of the TV easier. If sleeping in a recliner is a favorite activity, plenty of warm blankets and pillows can make it even more comfortable. Store the blankets and pillows in a trunk (used as a coffee table), so they can be accessible to you later. (AgingInPlace.org, 2022d)

Be Comfortable In The Living Room

Being comfortable in the living room is very important when getting older, as it can be more difficult to regulate body temperature correctly. Consider how to heat and cool the space effectively. To save money on the electric bill, turn the systems off or buy a single window a/c unit, a fan in the warmer months, a single electric heater, or a small electric fireplace to use in cooler months. (AgingInPlace.org, 2022d)

Staying Cool

A whole-house air conditioner may be necessary for areas of the country where it gets boiling in the summer. There are ductless options if the price of putting a whole house air conditioner in may be beyond the budget. A ductless cooling system allows for cooling in one or more rooms. The same is true with heat, a smaller heater in the living room, even if a whole-house furnace, is not an option. (AgingInPlace.org, 2022d)

Staying Warm

Electric heaters or small electric fireplaces are good choices because they are solid, stationary, have no flame to worry about, and are sealed units that do not get too hot to burn someone. The extra heat in the living room from a small electric fireplace will make it warmer in the winter. It will be cool, comfortable in the summer, and safe and secure all year round, the best of all worlds. (AgingInPlace.org, 2022d)

Keeping up with Hobbies In The Living Room

Many people like to read or participate in other hobbies in the living room. Hobbies may change or continue to be the same. Consider a hobby that can be done in the living room. Adapting to the surroundings and enjoying hobbies in the living room is possible. If reading is a favorite pastime, include a bookshelf or two in the living room design. If knitting or crocheting is enjoyable, having a basket of yarn and other supplies next to a favorite spot on the couch is a great idea. Using a computer or tablet in the living room is also great; consider using them where they can charge. (AgingInPlace.org, 2022d)

How To Make A Living Room Easy to Clean

Plenty of options make cleaning easier. Hard floors are easier to clean than carpeted floors. Vertical window blinds are easier to clean and collect less dust than horizontal ones. The living room's couches and chairs must be covered in stain-resistant fabric. Overall, there are many options for keeping things cleaner. (AgingInPlace.org, 2022d)

In this chapter, I discussed ways to design your living room so you can age-in-place, safely and easily as possible. You learned how to arrange furniture to avoid falling and tripping hazards, and you learned efficient ways to keep comfortable throughout the year and ways to keep the room clean.

The next chapter will discuss making a kitchen that is more accessible to everyone.

7

A KITCHEN FOR EVERYONE

When planning to stay at home for the long haul, consider personal safety and convenience issues in the kitchen, where we spend a lot of time. It is also one of the most dangerous rooms in a house. (Aging in Place, 2022b)

Hazards in the Kitchen

In research from Aging in Place (2022b), the following statistics are just a few reasons the kitchen is the most dangerous room in a home.

- 90% of kitchen washcloths failed cleanliness tests.

- Food-borne diseases cause 76 million cases of illness in the United States alone, according to the Centers for Disease Control and Prevention (CDC).

- There are over 150,000 kitchen cooking fires yearly.

- Cuts from kitchen tools account for 42% of hand injuries that ERs see.

- A home is twice as likely to have a fire without a fire alarm. -according to the U.S. Fire Administration.
- From 2002-2005, unattended cooking equipment accounted for 45% of home fatalities.

- Thirty-four fatal burn injuries occur yearly from kitchen burns.

- After age 65, falling becomes the leading cause of death in the home.

Falling is a cause of injury preventable by making home modifications with that hazard in mind. For seniors, avoiding falls means avoiding additional health problems. (Aging in Place, 2022b)

The Location of the Kitchen

Open-plan living is all the rage, and for excellent reason. Kitchens should open out to a dining and lounge room wherever possible. Ideally, a kitchen should connect to the entertaining outdoor area. That area could be located at the house's front, back, or side, but the best kitchen position will be close. Most kitchens have at least one wall of floor-to-ceiling cabinetry with no space for windows. Think carefully about which side of the room to install this wall, and choose the side with the least amount of natural light (if you can). Let in the maximum natural light in the kitchen. (Renovations, 2018)

Extra Room for Maneuverability

. . .

A kitchen should not be cramped. Everyone should have room to move around. The kitchen should have additional (42-48 inches) clearance around all doorways and pathways. (Aging in Place, 2022b)

Flooring

No matter the budget, make the flooring in the kitchen and elsewhere in the house a top priority. Any floor covering chosen should be non-glare. Moreover, do not have "throw" rugs on any floor because they pose a tripping hazard! Ideally, all flooring on the first floor of any home should be the same to prevent 'transitional' curbs that separate rooms. Flooring must prevent slipping accidents and maintain comfort for the feet. Vinyl, wood, or linoleum flooring are the best kitchen floor options. Hardwood or luxury vinyl plank is much easier to roll a wheelchair over a carpet. (Aging in Place, 2022b)

Kitchen Lighting

- Proper lighting helps to prevent accidents, creates a more suitable work environment, and reduces eye strain. Ensure that lighting in the kitchen reaches wherever it needs to be, especially in high-use kitchen areas. (Aging in Place, 2022b)

- Under-cabinet lighting illuminates work areas that would otherwise be dark. Task, track, or under cabinet lighting ensures anyone has appropriate light, no matter where they choose to work. (Aging in Place, 2022b)

- Recessed lights are a great way to illuminate a kitchen. Most modern light bulbs are LED. LED Light bulbs get the same power for a fraction of the energy use of traditional incandescent lights. (Aging in Place, 2022b)

- Many people install pendant-style lights over their kitchen islands and their main sink. Pendant lights are gorgeous; be cautious about the length of the chain that holds them. Ensure the chain is the proper size to not bump a head on the light fixture (if the chain is too long). Ensure the chain is not too short to get the required lighting.

Light Switch

Light switches need to be easy to use and accessible for guests. A light switch should be near the kitchen entrance and within arm's reach. A rocker-type light switch is usually the most convenient. Another popular kitchen light switch is an automatic light switch that turns on and off as a person enters or exits the kitchen. (Aging in Place, 2022b)

The color choice for the surfaces will influence how well the lighting works. Although cabinets and countertops should show their edges with bright colors, ensure those colors are not shiny. (Aging in Place, 2022b)

Outlets

When building a new home or remodeling a kitchen, make sure there are plenty of outlets in the kitchen. There is no reason to have more than two appliances plugged into a single outlet. Having more than two appliances plugged into one outlet increases the chances of an electrical accident. (Aging in Place, 2022b)

.   .   .

Kitchen Windows and Window Treatments

Kitchen windows should increase the amount of natural light in the room. Protect everyone's privacy with easily accessible blinds, ensuring the throw string is long enough to reach easily without becoming a slip-and-fall hazard. (Aging in Place, 2022b)

Accessible Thermostat in the Kitchen

Ensure an easy-to-use thermostat or fan is within easy reach in case the kitchen gets too hot. Helping to eliminate the possibility of lightheadedness or fainting from overheating or heat exhaustion. (Aging in Place, 2022b)

Cabinet Doors and Drawers and Appliance Handles

Something as easy as finding the right cabinet door or drawer handle can be tricky as a person gets older or has trouble with finger dexterity. Choosing a pull handle that gives a person a better grip should be on all cabinets, appliances, and entry doors leading into the room. (Aging in Place, 2022b)

Kitchen Cabinets

A Pull-Down Shelf in Upper Cabinets

Cabinets should not be difficult to reach. If the upper cabinets are exceptionally tall, consider adding a pull-out step around the floor's perimeter. A pull-down shelf in upper cabinets helps people get the items they need. (Aging in Place, 2022b)

Roll-Out Shelf in Lower Cabinets

In general, installing a roll-out shelf in lower cabinets is the way to go in a kitchen. A roll-out shelf reduces back strain, maximizes storage space in the lower cabinets, and makes it easy to access the items in the back of the cabinet. Roll-out shelving also provides additional safety measures for people who may have trouble reaching the items on the shelf. Cabinets with pull-out shelves are found at any major home improvement store or have them built in through a custom cabinet. (Aging in Place, 2022b)

Kitchen Countertop

Multi-Height Countertops

The average countertop height is 36 inches off the floor. However, heights can vary from 35 1/2" to 37", depending on cabinet height and the counter's thickness. A below-average countertop height is 32". One above average is 38"-39". A countertop height that works best for someone who uses a wheelchair or scooter may be between 31 to 34inches high. (Ganea, 2022)

The Benefits Of Having A Countertop at Various Heights

One size fits all rarely works, and countertops are a good example. Since standard heights do not work for everybody, the solution often is to have a countertop at a custom height. Multi-height counters are an excellent solution for a family. They feature surfaces at different heights so everyone can feel comfortable using the kitchen. A bar-height table works well with bar stools but is not the most comfortable or safest option for everyone to eat. A lower counter brings the eating area to a more comfortable level. (Ganea, 2022)

Automatic Height-Adjustable Countertop

An automatic height-adjustable kitchen countertop can be ideal for a multi-generational or multi-ability household. The goal is to provide an optimal, safe working environment for standing and seated users. The lift system permits up-down movement of the countertop. They are suited for both new builds and remodels. (AIPatHome.com, 2014)

There are three different methods available for raising and lowering the kitchen components:

- electric push-button
- manual,
- bracket-mounted

An electric or manual (crank) version of an adjustable countertop is best if you often need to adjust the countertop height. Use the bracket-mounted version for occasional height adjustments. (AIPatHome.com, 2014)

These lifting devices have safety systems to ensure no one gets pinched or crushed by the countertop. Aesthetic covers conceal electric service lines, water supply, and disposal tubing. (AIPatHome.com, 2014)

· · ·

Use an adjustable height system that has a sink and cooktop on the countertop. The reason is; is that those two items are the most used in the kitchen by most people of various heights. A stovetop and sink that are closer together are nice because there are fewer steps to take. There is a prep space between the two. If strength or mobility is an issue, having a cooktop next to a sink will allow a pot to slide effortlessly across the countertop from the sink to the stovetop.

Edges on Countertops

Sharp corners or edges of a countertop tend to cause more injuries; countertops with rounded corners and edges are best. A professional opinion can help configure safe countertops with ease of use, easy maintenance, and relativity clutter-free. (Aging in Place, 2022b)

Kitchen Appliances

Oven, Cooktop, Sink, Refrigerator, Freezer, and Dishwasher

There are a lot of appliances in a kitchen. In this chapter, I will focus on describing the six appliances in most kitchens. First, let's discuss the oven, cooktop, sink, refrigerator, and freezers.

Place the oven, cooktop, sink, and refrigerator as close to each other as possible. Forming a "work triangle" between the frequently used kitchen appliances prevents wasting time during prep, cooking, and cleanup. (Aging in Place, 2022b)

1. Wall Oven

The wall oven is the most versatile, convenient, and safe version of a range available in a home. It is best to have a wall oven mounted at a level where anyone can easily reach it. The wall oven can also be aligned with the adjacent countertop, reducing the need to bend or lift. Choose a wall oven with a large function display that is easy to see. The latest wall ovens are also self-cleaning, so one no longer needs to bend down to clean it. It is a great idea to install a pull-out counter directly underneath the oven, making it easy to get hot dishes out. (Aging in Place, 2022b)

2. Cooktop

A cooktop is also safer for the home. A cooktop close to a water source makes it easier to fill pots more conveniently. Cooktops cool off much faster and can be installed at various heights to ensure comfort, whether sitting or standing. Cooktops with front-mounted controls are the safest because they keep people from leaning over hot burners. (Aging in Place, 2022b)

• **Roll-Under (Accessible) Cooktop**

The easiest way to make a cooktop accessible (to people who use a walker or wheelchair or need to sit down while cooking) is to install cabinet doors directly underneath. Ideally, a motorized sink or adjustable height countertop offers the freedom of independent adjustment, particularly for people who use a walker or wheelchair. If considering a motorized sink, leave space below the sink to allow wheelchair access. (Aging in Place, 2022b)

3. **Kitchen Sink**

Consider the depth of the sink in the kitchen. Make sure that the sink is around 6-11 inches deep. This depth may seem shallow, but the depth prevents someone from bending over too far to reach the drain. (Aging in Place, 2022b)

Saladino, A. (2022) compiled below a list of kitchen sinks types ranging between style and material.

14 TYPES OF KITCHEN SINKS

1. SINGLE-BOWL SINK

A single-bowl sink feature one large basin making cleaning large pots and pans easy because they can lay flat at the bottom of the sink. (Saladino, 2022)

2. DOUBLE-BOWL SINK

Double-basin sinks offer both functionality and style. These sinks feature a divider to designate one side for washing dishes and the other for drying, or food prep. (Saladino, 2022)

3. OVER-MOUNT KITCHEN SINK

An over-mount sink, also known as a drop-in sink, drops into the counter, creating a lip or rim around the sink is easy to install and provides extra support. (Saladino, 2022)

4. UNDER-MOUNT SINK

An under-mount is installed directly under the counter, creating a seamless look from countertop to sink. This type of sink looks sleek, making cleanup easy as debris can be pushed now into the sink. (Saladino, 2022)

. . .

5. STAINLESS STEEL SINK

A stainless steel sink is light, easy to install, and a practical and popular option and comes in various styles, such as farmhouse, under-mount, and over-mount. These sinks are expensive, but they are more affordable compared to other high-quality materials like granite. Manufacturers use sheet thickness to categorize a stainless steel sink. A thicker gauge means a sink will be heavier and cheaper; a thinner gauge means a sink is lighter and often more expensive. Stainless steel sinks are noisier than other sink materials and can dent but offer excellent heat and stain resistance. (Saladino, 2022)

6. CAST IRON SINK

Cast iron sinks sprayed with a porcelain enamel coating give them a glossy white finish. This coating appeals to many homeowners looking for a sink to complement their vintage, farmhouse, or country-style kitchen. Cast iron sinks are heavier and more durable than others, but the porcelain enamel can chip easily. Do not clean these sinks with abrasive cleaners, as they will wear down the enamel coating. Use caution when washing dishes because the sink's hardness can easily chip the dishware. (Saladino, 2022)

. . .

7. FIRECLAY SINK

A Fireclay sink is made from fusing clay and a glaze at very high temperatures. Fireclay sinks are identical to cast iron sinks but are more durable. They will not chip, etch, or stain, and abrasive cleaners can clean the sink. Fireclay sinks are more expensive than cast iron due to the more extensive fabrication process. (Saladino, 2022)

8. GRANITE SINK

A Granite sink is constructed by gluing crushed granite with a resin filler. This type of sink is durable, stain-resistant, and provides a cutting-edge modern look to any kitchen. This sink is also quieter than other sinks due to its density. A granite composite sink is heavier than stainless steel sinks, so add extra support to accommodate its weight. (Saladino, 2022)

9. FARMHOUSE SINK

A farmhouse-style sink extends over the counter. Most commonly used in a traditional, rustic, or modern farmhouse-style kitchen and can be a single or double bowl. These durable sinks typically come as fireclay or cast iron and are easy to clean. A deep basin makes them perfect for oversized pots and pans, providing easy cleanup. A portion of the counter has to be cut, making them pricey and more difficult to install. (Saladino, 2022)

10. CORNER SINK

Corner sinks are double-basin sinks installed in the corner of a counter. The two basins are set in a catty-corner manner. This unique design can be helpful if looking to maximize counter space. Since most counters come together at the corner, custom cuts in the counter will add to the cost of installing this type of sink. (Saladino, 2022)

11. KITCHEN ISLAND SINK

Kitchen islands are increasing in popularity, and so are incorporating a sink in that island. Depending on user needs, these sinks can be primary or prep sinks. Kitchen island sinks complement workflow and saves space on the main counter. They can also turn a kitchen island into a complete workspace. They look beautiful on wood, granite, or stainless steel island, so the design options are endless. When adding a sink to a kitchen island, consider the extra costs of installing plumbing on the kitchen island. (Saladino, 2022)

12. BAR SINK

Bar sinks installed in a wet bar or kitchen island are smaller and more shallow than the average kitchen sink, making them a secondary option. They are typically a single-bowl design for prep work, drink-making, and convenient cleanup. When entertaining a large family or friends, a bar sink is excellent in a home bar, patio, or terrace. (Saladino, 2022)

13. KITCHEN SINK WITH AN ATTACHED DRAINBOARD

This stainless steel sink with an attached apron (the drainboard) allows water to drain directly into the sink, making them practical and eco-friendly. A drainboard sink is excellent if someone loves to cook because they create a counter's designated food prep section. The drainboard provides a spot to dry dishes and other kitchenware by allowing excess water to flow directly into the sink. This method leaves cleaner counters and saves energy by not using a dishwasher to wash and dry dishes. (Saladino, 2022)

14. INTEGRATED KITCHEN SINK

An integrated kitchen sink can serve as a statement piece in a kitchen if a customized option is wanted. These sinks are integrated within a countertop and constructed of the same material - in most cases, in one piece -

providing a sleek and seamless look. However, this sink style can be costly compared to other kitchen sinks. (Saladino, 2022)

A sink is just a decorative bowl without a faucet. So, let's talk about the eight types of kitchen sink faucets Homestratosphere's Editorial Staff & Writers (2021b) describe below.

The 8 Main Types of Kitchen Sink Faucets

1. The Pull Down Faucet

This primary type of faucet has a pull-down faucet with a curve that can pull straight into the sink. This faucet works well for cleaning dishes, products, and even a new puppy! The pull-down feature makes for a beautiful cleanup of that messy sink. (Homestratosphere's Editorial Staff & Writers, 2021b)

2. The Pull-Out Faucet

A pull-out faucet has a body that works in a straight line. In contrast, a pull-out faucet can pull down straight into the sink. This option allows for 360-degree spraying potential. (Homestratosphere's Editorial Staff & Writers, 2021b)

3. The Single-Handle Faucet

A single-handle faucet uses one lever to position water temperature from left to right. Pulling the lever up or down controls water pressure. Getting the water to the desired temperature can take a little time. It will usually be less precise when the water temperature is too cold or too hot. (Homestratosphere's Editorial Staff & Writers, 2021b)

The Benefits of A Single Handle Faucet

A single-lever faucet handles the water control and water temperature. A pull-out spray nozzle can be installed on this type of faucet. One water plumbing line is attached to the handle and nozzle, so both hot and cold water comes out of one faucet body. Only one hole is needed on a countertop, making for the most straightforward installation. A single-handle faucet is easier to maneuver with one hand, so finding the appropriate temperature is easy. Since a single-handle faucet only needs one entryway into the countertop, this also makes for easier cleaning! (Lentz, 2022)

. . .

Cons: This type of faucet tends to experience more leaks than the double-handle faucet, as more water pressure comes from one output. If a single-handle faucet ever leaks, the water must be off to have it fixed, leaving the sink without water access until it gets fixed. (Lentz, 2022)

4. The Dual-Handle Faucet

A dual-handle has separate levers for warm and cool water. Sometimes, the two handles attach to the same central piece; in other cases, they are a few inches apart. Either way, they would be on the sides of the main tap. This faucet requires separate connections to hot and cold water. The right handle controls hot water, and the left controls cold water. Bringing the handle towards the center will control water pressure. (Homestratosphere's Editorial Staff & Writers, 2021b)

5. The Commercial Style Faucet

A commercial-style faucet uses a more extended, flexible design. Depending on the chosen model, multiple taps for different needs might exist. This faucet creates a more modern appearance in a home or professional kitchen. Any guest brought over will think there is a serious chef. (Homestratosphere's Editorial Staff & Writers, 2021b)

. . .

6. The Separate Spray Faucet

A separate spray faucet might be ideal when looking for something more flexible. This faucet has a different handle with a trigger to avert the water from the primary faucet to the spray nozzle. The spray nozzle will be active when turning on the standard tap, as water comes to the tap without problems. (Homestratosphere's Editorial Staff & Writers, 2021b)

7. The Pot Filler Faucet

A pot-filler faucet has an arm extension that swivels out to go over a pot or large item in a sink. Some models are on a wall, linked to the plumbing system, and near a cooktop. (Homestratosphere's Editorial Staff & Writers, 2021b)

8. The Motion Detection Faucet

The last option is a faucet that places a hand, a pot, or a pan over a sensor to activate water flow. The sensor is in a dark spot near the middle part of the faucet. (Homestratosphere's Editorial Staff & Writers, 2021b)

The Motion Detection Faucet Pros and Cons

More and more motion sensor facets have been showing up in home kitchens or bathrooms. However, most households still have the traditional type. (Homestratosphere's Editorial Staff & Writers, 2021a)

Pros

- Sensor faucets have a low flow rate, materials that prevent leakage, and a valve that would be closed by default which conserves water. (Homestratosphere's Editorial Staff & Writers, 2021a)

- Each sensor faucet saves more energy than traditional faucets, benefiting the environment if power comes from a renewable source and if restraints control the water outflow. (Homestratosphere's Editorial Staff & Writers, 2021a)

- The faucet will help to achieve a cleaner bathroom since sink overflow will reduce water splashes. The user's dirty hands will not come into contact with the faucet due to its self-closing mechanism, guaranteeing less water contamination. (Homestratosphere's Editorial Staff & Writers, 2021a)

Cons

- The price of a sensor faucet is reasonable enough. However, the faucet may need more initial investment than traditional taps. It may be problematic for those on a budget, but a sensor faucet saves more money in the long run. People who move a lot will not appreciate the cost-effectiveness of a sensor faucet for years. (Homestratosphere's Editorial Staff & Writers, 2021a)

- Accidental activation of a sensor-type faucet does occur. So this type of faucet is not recommended for homeowners with pets since small cats or dogs can walk on a sink countertop and activate the tap, wasting water and energy. (Homestratosphere's Editorial Staff & Writers, 2021a)

- Sensor faucets run on electricity, so there will be no water if there is a power outage. Suppose a home is in an area that usually experiences power outages from storms. In that case, sensor taps are not the right choice. (Homestratosphere's Editorial Staff & Writers, 2021a)

Homestratosphere's Editorial Staff & Writers (2021a) state the following facts about sensor faucets:

- The level of cross-contamination is lower than other faucets.

- A sensor faucet reduces the transmission of germs and bacteria.

- A sensor faucet is hygienic.

- Users of a sensor faucet conserve 70% of water.

- A sensor faucet requires less maintenance than other faucets.

- A sensor faucet is more durable and long-lasting.

Water Temp and Soap location

One of the essential features of a sink should be an anti-scald device. As stated before, many emergency room injuries are caused yearly by scalding water. A soap dispenser makes accessing soap easy. Cleaning materials in a dispenser also makes wiping countertops and scrubbing heavy pots that cannot go into the dishwasher easier. Cleanliness is essential to avoid food poisoning and other diseases. Cleaning materials in individually labeled bottles are not as convenient as having them in a single location by the sink. (Aging in Place, 2022b)

Refrigerator And Freezer

When researching the perfect fridge and freezer for you, there are features to look at. First, a refrigerator or freezer with a long door handle allows someone to open them easier. Secondly, look at how much space is available for food, drinks, and condiments. Third, consider interior lighting that illuminates features like water and ice dispensers; and choose the best option.

(Aging in Place, 2022b)

Refrigerator Shelves

Slide-out shelves are easier to access than traditional shelving. These transparent shelves will provide additional perspective regardless of the refrigerator's approach. Spills are less likely to occur on transparent shelves that slide out. (Aging in Place, 2022b)

Types of Refrigerators and Freezers

1. Side-by-Side Refrigerator

Side-by-side refrigerator freezer units are the most accessible because both doors can open fully. These units have narrow doors, reducing the probability of injury because of the door swing radius. (Aging in Place, 2022b)

. . .

2. French Door Refrigerators

Stone, J. (2022) states that there are four main types of French door refrigerator designs:

- Original French Door Style: Two doors on top and one freezer drawer below.

- French Door with a Drawer: Two doors on top, a fridge drawer (in the middle), and a freezer drawer on the bottom.

- Four French Door. Two refrigerator doors on top and two freezer doors on the bottom.

- Two doors on top, two fridge drawers in the middle, and a freezer drawer at the bottom.

3. Top Freezer Refrigerators

A top freezer design was standard in the past; slightly smaller than other models and does not come with additional features—no water or ice dispenser in the door. A top freezer refrigerator is a straightforward appliance. (Stone, 2022)

4. Bottom Freezer Refrigerators

Refrigerators also come in arrangements with a freezer on the bottom. High-end fridge models have started to place the freezer drawer on the bottom, accessed via a slide-out drawer. This design is similar to the French door models, with just a single swing-out door on top. (Stone, 2022)

5. Column Refrigerators

Column refrigerators are slowly growing in popularity. They are a tall, separate built-in fridge and freezer. The refrigerator and freezer may be next to each other (the typical arrangement) or in different kitchen areas. (Stone, 2022)

6. Chest Freezers or Upright Freezers

Freezer-only appliances can be in an upright (with a swing door) or chest design. They are a second freezer for additional storage, then programmed to low temperatures for deep-freezing foods to preserve them for long periods. Found in basements, garages, or storage spaces. (Stone, 2022)

7. Compact Refrigerators

Compact refrigerators are smaller than standard refrigerators but larger than mini-fridges. They are ideal for small spaces, like apartments or custom-designed kitchens. These appliances are easy to build into a kitchen design and fit into cabinets, resulting in a streamlined look. When considering a compact refrigerator, choose one large enough to fit everything needed; they are still limited in space. (Stone, 2022)

8. Mini-Fridges

The mini-fridge offers an excellent solution for additional cold storage in a compact refrigerator. An advantage of a mini fridge is that it takes up less home space and costs less to purchase and operate than a full-sized fridge. Mini-refrigerators can be everywhere. Under a desk, kitchen counter, in-home bars, garages, home theaters, or other dedicated spaces for stocking drinks, snacks, or other products that need to be cold. Mini fridges can come as free-standing units or built-in models. (Stone, 2022)

. . .

9. Wine Refrigerators

Suppose the purpose of buying a refrigerator is to keep wine accessible, chilled, and fresh. In that case, consider a wine fridge. There are many wine refrigerators, including under-counter designs and full-size models that can hold up to 180 bottles. These refrigerators are great for showcasing a prized wine collection and entertaining guests. (Stone, 2022)

10. Under-counter Refrigerator Drawers

Use the main fridge for overstock and these drawers as the go-to place for prep ingredients. The drawers keep needed food for recipes on hand and accessible. Accessibility is a significant benefit of this type of fridge. Refrigerated or freezer drawers are accessible for kids and those who use wheelchairs. Under-counter refrigerators provide room for essential cabinet and countertop storage when designing a small kitchen. The main drawbacks of these specialty fridges are that they are expensive and do not substitute for a full-size refrigerator. (Stone, 2022)

9 Types of Dishwashers

1. Built-in Dishwashers

Built-in dishwashers are directly connected to the plumbing and can be used immediately. (Bowen, 2021b)

2. Countertop Dishwashers

The countertop dishwasher is the solution for having a dishwasher in a small space. (Bowen, 2021b)

3. Top-control Dishwashers

These dishwashers have flat, practically invisible control buttons (located on the top of the dishwasher), allowing the machine to blend well in the kitchen. (Bowen, 2021b)

4. Front-control Dishwashers

The visible front control panel makes the dishwasher practical and accessible. (Bowen, 2021b)

5. Integrated Dishwashers

These dishwashers provide a streamlined look while still being functional. The disadvantage is that the machine is stationary. If the dishwasher breaks, fixing it will be challenging. (Bowen, 2021b)

. . .

6. Semi-integrated Dishwashers

These dishwashers offer the best of both worlds, a streamlined look just like integrated dishwashers, and fixing it will be easier. (Bowen, 2021b)

7. Freestanding Dishwashers

These types of dishwashers can be portable or built-in. Freestanding dishwashers stand out in a kitchen. However, these dishwashers are easy to operate and be moved easily. (Bowen, 2021b)

8. Portable Dishwashers

These dishwashers do not require a dedicated space in the kitchen. The dishwasher also offers a portable countertop space, which is excellent if extra space is needed. The portability does come with a cost; however, the dishwashers' ability to handle loads is limited. (Bowen, 2021b)

9. Drawer-style Dishwashers

These dishwashers load and unload the dishes (from the top)—no need to bend over to access from the dishwasher's front. A drawer-style dishwasher is convenient for someone who has back problems or has issues bending over. This dishwasher is one unit. It can be bought as one unit and installed at a convenient height, or two can be purchased together and stacked on top. This dishwasher style is a state-of-the-art dishwasher and one that is easy on the body; consider the drawer-style dishwashers. (Bowen, 2021b)

No matter the type or style of dishwasher chosen, ensure that it is at a convenient height for the people who use it the most often.

Safety in the Kitchen

Unattended Cooking Appliances

Most modern kitchen appliances with safety features will come with automatic shut-off options helping to prevent accidents. A kitchen appliance that shut off automatically eliminates the possibility of an unattended device causing accidental fires or other injuries in the kitchen. (Aging in Place, 2022b)

Medical Alert Device

A medical alert device allows someone to notify medical personnel if an accident should occur. The alert devices should be in multiple places around the house, but the kitchen must be a place for at least one. (Aging in Place, 2022b)

Smoke and Monoxide Detectors

Smoke and carbon monoxide detectors should be throughout the house and close to the kitchen. (Aging in Place, 2022b)

Having a smoke alarm that "speaks" to you when it goes off; is quite helpful to anyone who is vision impaired (which is everyone in a fire).

Fire Extinguisher

An up-to-date fire extinguisher that is easy to use should always be close to the kitchen. Everyone must know where it is and how to use it. (Aging in Place, 2022b)

Step stools and Helpful Kitchen Utensils

A step stool will help get to top-level cabinets. If possible, install the step stool with wall attachments rather than separate stools that might be tripped over if forgotten. (Aging in Place, 2022b)

Special utensils help users provide additional functionality. Look for "inclusive designed" utensils that are easier to use, safer, and more convenient at any age. (Aging in Place, 2022b)

Microwave

Many modern microwaves have "smart" features to benefit people who are hard of hearing or visually impaired. A loud beep indicates when the food needs stirring, reheating, or done. The best microwaves also have simple controls with large, easily read labels or captions. Be sure to install the microwave oven at an accessible height. (Aging in Place, 2022b)

An Accessible Workstation

Incorporating a workstation accessible to people regardless of age or ability is vital in a kitchen. Keeping a microwave, blender, toaster, etc., at a height that is easily accessible ensures that those appliances will be used independently by all.

A Kitchen That is Usable by Everyone

A functional kitchen is helpful, especially for someone with limited mobility, motor, or cognitive limitations. The best way to respect the needs and abilities of each person who lives in a home or may visit is to provide kitchen solutions to their specific needs. (Aging in Place, 2022b)

In this chapter, I talked about ways to design a kitchen so you can age in place safely and efficiently. I write about safety, location, having space to move around, and different types of safety flooring. I also wrote about types of kitchen lighting, light switches and outlets, window treatment, and the importance of easy-to-use thermostats within reach. Next was cabinet handles, cabinets, kitchen appliances, sinks, and faucets. Finally, I wrote about maintaining safety and independence in the kitchen.

Next Chapter, you will learn how to make your main bedroom and closet accessible to you as you age.

EVERYTHING YOU WANTED TO KNOW ABOUT DESIGNING THE MAIN BEDROOM AND CLOSET AND WERE AFRAID TO ASK

Avoiding safety hazards in the bedroom may be low on your list of priorities. But if you think about it, a lot of time is spent in your main bedroom, over 24 hours. Time is spent in the bedroom, getting ready for the day and getting ready for bed. Entire days may be spent in the bedroom during illness or injury. Navigating a bedroom in the dark would be necessary during this time. Planning a safe, comfortable bedroom is a good idea to age in place successfully. (AgingInPlace.org 2022a)

Here are a few suggestions from Aging In Place (2022a) about bedroom placement and safety.

Second-floor main bedroom

Almost seven million Americans use some assistance device (a cane, walker, scooter, wheelchair, or crutches) for mobility. For these individuals, stairs and multi-story homes are a challenge. Even if no assistance is required to walk or maneuver up and down stairs, NOW is the time for a remodeling or building plan to include a main bedroom suite on the first floor. (AgingInPlace.org 2022a)

Stairlifts

Although, if a ground-floor bedroom is not an option, consider installing a home stair lift to access the main bedroom. Stairlifts benefit people with physical mobility problems, heart and lung issues, and other challenges. Before a stair lift is installed, please consider how the stair lift fits in a stairway, how much adjustability the lift has, and how the lift is controlled by remote control functions or the push of a button. (AgingInPlace.org 2022a)

A Standing Platform

Different stair lifts may offer better comfort and ease of use. A stair lift with a standing platform will benefit someone who has problems bending their knees; they are narrower than a full-seated lift and have a seat, footrest, and control button. (AgingInPlace.org 2022a)

A perch-style seat on a stair lift does not require a person to bend their legs and is suitable for people who have knee issues. Other stair lifts offer a fold-up seat for multi-person homes and seniors with declining mobility (AgingIn-Place.org 2022a)

Bedroom Safety

A lot of time is spent in the bedroom. A safer bedroom can help maintain independence and decrease the risk of life-threatening accidents. So planning for safety is the number one priority. (AgingInPlace.org 2022a)

To remain safe, one must declutter the bedroom space and clear pathways to ensure movement through the room is more accessible. Remove area rugs: loose rugs put seniors at risk for falls and injuries. In addition, check the room's carpeting. If the carpeting is damaged or has curled-up edges, it can pose a tripping risk. (AgingInPlace.org 2022a)

When remodeling or building a house to age in place, consider the following questions from Aging In Place (2022a) regarding safety in your bedroom:

- Is there a clear clutter-free pathway from the bedroom to the ensuite bathroom?
- Do the windows have secure screens and locks?
- Can windows be used easily by people with arthritis and visual impairments?
- Is all the furniture sturdy
- Are items used daily within easy reach?

- Are electronics and medical equipment (with cords and cables) secured and placed out of the way?

Follow all home care instructions and safety protocols for medical equipment kept in the bedroom. (AgingInPlace.org 2022a)

* * *

The Bed and Other Furniture In The Main Bedroom

Aging in place requires planning and thinking about the bed and other furniture in the main bedroom. Sleep patterns change as people age, and some find falling and staying asleep difficult. To remain safe, avoid a bed skirt or any bedspread, comforter, or duvet that reaches the floor. A foot can get tangled in these bedclothes, resulting in a fall. (AgingInPlace.org 2022a)

An Adjustable Bed

The perfect time to replace a bed is during the main bedroom remodel. A new adjustable bed may be in your future and will make aging in place safer. This type of bed looks like a standard one, but the head and feet raise and lower to obtain a comfortable, custom sleep position. Some of these beds have a massage feature, a wireless hand control, and the ability to adjust the mattresses' firmness. (AgingIn-Place.org 2022a)

If your current bed serves its purpose, offers comfort, and a good night's sleep, replacing it will not be necessary. If this is the case, but personal safety is still a concern, put a mat on the floor at the side of the bed to add protection in case you fall. Also, installing a motion-sensor light (under the bed) will offer much-needed light to see at night before you leave the bed. (AgingInPlace.org 2022a)

New Bedding and Bed Height

Finally, new bedding may be needed for a bedroom remodel. If new bedding comes with a bed, ensure that your feet do not get tangled in these bedclothes. Consider getting a mattress protector as well. A mattress protector prevents odor or wetness issues. Ensure a mattress protector is laundered regularly to stay fresh and clean. One final note: when considering whether to keep an old bed (or when looking at new bed models), remember that the safest bed sits between 20-23 inches from the floor. (AgingInPlace.org 2022a)

Sturdy Furniture

Consider other bedroom furnishings (as you plan to age in place) because they can also raise safety concerns. To avoid accidents, ensure all bedroom furniture (bookshelves and wardrobes) is sturdy and anchored to the wall. Place non-skid pads under nightstands, dressers, and any other room furniture to prevent them from scratching the floor and keep them in place. (AgingInPlace.org 2022a)

* * *

Flooring

The best bedroom flooring minimizes slipping and sliding by humans and furniture. Suitable flooring also is easy for a person to move their wheelchair, scooter, walker, or cane across. A floor in a bedroom should be easy to keep clean to allow the most significant independence possible while you age. The flooring choice will depend on budget, décor preferences, and any physical limitations or restrictions you have. (AgingInPlace.org 2022a)

Aging In place (2022a) states some of the most popular options for flooring and the pros and cons of each. (Aging In Place, 2022)

Hardwood

Hardwood floors are beautiful but can damage by any spilled liquid. Depending on the finish of the hardwood, they can also create a falling hazard by making slips more likely. If you choose hardwood, avoid using area rugs or tape down their edges to minimize the risk of falling. (AgingInPlace.org 2022a)

Laminate Flooring

A laminate floor is an alternative to traditional hardwood; it is easy to clean, resistant to stains, and less expensive than hardwood to install. However, they can present similar safety issues to hardwood floors, so take the appropriate precautions. (AgingInPlace.org 2022a)

Carpet

Carpet seems like an obvious solution, but it comes with challenges. Carpet may make it difficult to use a mobility assistance device like a walker or cane. Carpet fibers hold onto allergens that increase respiratory issues for people suffering from allergies. (AgingInPlace.org 2022a)

Main Bedroom Lighting

Proper lighting provides safety and health benefits and makes the space more aesthetically pleasing. (AgingInPlace.org 2022a)

Seeing Better

The Lighting Research Center et al. (2001) experts state that eyesight changes as a person ages. Seeing distances, color perception, and discrimination is difficult for older adults. High illumination levels provided by lamps (as opposed to traditional lights) help older adults see and distinguish colors better. Proper lighting helps to choose clothes that match and to enjoy reading.

Balance Light Levels In The Main Bedroom

If one part of the bedroom is dim while the other is bright, that could mean problems with glare. It also can mean older eyes may take more time to change to see darker areas safely. (The Lighting Research Center et al., 2001)

The Lighting Research Center

The Lighting Research Center at the Rensselaer Polytechnic Institute has developed these principles to guide people to light their homes.

The Lighting Research Center (LRC) suggests these other lighting options for the bedroom:

- Lighter paint on walls to minimize shadows
- Have a lamp that turns on when it is touched
- Have light switches that are 'rocker' style (that glow in the dark) and are easy to use
- Have motion-sensor night lights in the bedroom.

Ambient and Task Light

Ambient lighting is a ceiling light, table lamp, or wall sconce. Task lighting is more concentrated and focused, essential for reading, applying makeup, and where more focus is needed. The best option is to mount a lamp on a swing arm above the headboard so the light hits below eye level to help avoid eye strain when reading. Lights that are too bright are as bad as lights that are too dim. Ensure there is no chance of temporary blindness when an older person enters the room and turns on the lights. (AgingInPlace.org 2022a)

* * *

Technology, Cords, and Cables

Technology today enables individuals to do so much more independently and has the potential to make aging in place more accessible and safer. Using electronics has become an essential daily part of life. When looking to age in place, be aware that cables that come with technology can turn into tripping hazards. Ensure all cords are out of high-traffic areas. Be aware any frayed or damaged electrical cord is a fire hazard; act now to replace any older cables in the bedroom and the house. (AgingInPlace.org 2022a)

An electrician can place outlets in convenient locations (by nightstands, in a corner, or even in the middle of a wall for a future television) to eliminate having electrical cords every-where. That's also an opportunity to raise outlets to reduce tripping over cords. Eliminating the need to bend over and plug in a cable is helpful and essential to anyone with mobility or other physical issues. (AgingInPlace.org 2022a)

Ensure the room has Wi-Fi access and that device charging stations are easy to reach and use. The ease of use is not just for convenience: today's technology enables individuals to do more independently and makes aging in place safer. Since every person and their needs are unique, thoroughly researching the many tech options available is critical. (AgingInPlace.org 2022a)

Phone Access

Communication is essential. A bedroom should have a phone next to the bed. The phone should be easy to handle, have a backlit keypad, and have a large screen. A phone makes reaching family, friends, and emergency assistance easier. Have a backup battery charger available in case of a power outage. A person should not lose the ability to communicate during a power outage. Keep a paper copy of all numbers programmed in all phones if the numbers disappear from a cell phone. Keep a copy in a nightstand drawer and a copy in a family member's home in case the others are misplaced. (AgingInPlace.org 2022a)

Accessories and Finishes

Select accessories that reflect an upbeat personality to ensure that the main bedroom feels cozy, personal, and inviting. So go ahead and put framed pictures of family and friends on the nightstand. (AgingInPlace.org 2022a)

Digital Clock

Have a digital clock that is visible from the bed. This clock may be wall-mounted or free-standing and placed on a bookshelf or a table. The bed should not have a lot of stylish throw pillows on it. Pillows may look great and welcoming, but where will the throw pillows go when you want to sleep?

The floor is neither a safe solution nor the foot of the bed, as stacked pillows may fall into the walkway. (AgingInPlace.org 2022a)

White noise generators

White noise generators (electronic devices that produce sound effects) like a gentle rain, running water, or a crashing surf—will contribute to better sleep quality by softening or even masking outside noise that might interfere with sleep. (AgingInPlace.org 2022a)

Automated or Motorized Window Coverings

Automated or motorized window coverings are controlled from the bed or anywhere in the room using a remote control. The remote lowers and raises the blinds or shades without getting out of bed. A remote for the window blind is a nice treat on a lazy morning and an asset to anyone who is bedridden or has mobility issues. Blackout-style blinds/shades will keep the room dark and improve sleep quality. (AgingInPlace.org 2022a)

The Main Bedroom Closet

Ideally, creating a "dream" main bedroom includes having a spacious, well-lit walk-in closet that has storage that's easy to reach. Hang a clothes bar 32 inches off the floor, at least in part of the closet. Make sure some of the storage shelves are accessible. It is a good idea not to store many items on the floor because of access issues (hard to bend over or in the way). The items on the closet shelves should be accessible and obtainable without struggle or a step stool. (AgingIn-Place.org 2022a)

Ensure a walk-in closet's doorway is 36 inches wide to accommodate a wheelchair or other mobility assistance device. A sliding door, barn door, pocket door, or even a fold-out door will add style to the room and ensure enough space to turn around. Installing a lever-style door knob or pull handle on the door will make it easy to open. (AgingIn-Place.org 2022a)

Keep the closet clutter-free. It is a good idea not to store many items on the floor because of access issues (hard to bend over or in the way). A lot of clutter on the floor makes it hard to find items and can increase the risk of tripping over things when the walkway needs to be used. Not only should you have a clutter-free closet floor, but you also should not put anything heavy on a shelf that may fall and cause an injury. (AgingInPlace.org 2022a)

Using Your Main Bedroom Closet as A Safe or Storm Shelter

If you are building a home without a basement (or adding an addition to your home), I recommend you use your main bedroom closet as a storm shelter or safe room accessible to everyone in the house and be big enough for four people.

Fregenal (2019b) shares the other requirements for safe rooms.

- A safe space should be on the ground floor or below ground.
- The doors and door frames should be steel or thick, heavy wood. A strong deadbolt lock is essential.
- The walls should be two layers of one-inch thick plywood.
- Safe rooms should have a ventilation shaft connected to the outdoors.

- If the room has no ventilation shaft, have a portable air filtration machine if you stay in the room for a long time; however, these machines require electricity, which might not be available in a catastrophe.
- The safe room must have fresh water, food supplies, and a portable hand-crank-powered radio. You must also have a (battery-operated) light, a cell phone charger, a first aid kit, and medical supplies. Chairs, cots, sleeping bags, and pillows should also be kept in the safe room.

Closet Lighting

The bedroom closet must have good lighting that makes it easy to see clothing, colors, and other items. Adding a lamp with a motion sensor will switch on and illuminate the area. (AgingInPlace.org 2022a)

* * *

In this chapter, I talked about ways to design the main bedroom to age in place safely and efficiently. I write about safety, the location of the main bedroom, and how to get upstairs if the main bedroom is on the second floor. I write about to importance of having enough space to move around and different types of flooring, decluttering the space.

I wrote about adjustable beds, bedding, lighting, sturdy furniture, window treatment, and the importance of easy-to-reach outlets and out-of-place electrical cords. Next was technology, accessories, and how to remodel (or build) the main bedroom closet into a storm shelter or safe room.

In the next Chapter, you will learn how to make your ensuite bedroom bathroom accessible as you age.

9

WHAT YOU CAN DO ABOUT DESIGNING AN ACCESSIBLE MAIN BEDROOM ENSUITE BATHROOM RIGHT NOW

Before you design your "dream" ensuite bathroom, think about your future health needs that might crop up. Designing a bathroom will take time and effort, and costs will be involved. In the end, having a comfortable and safe bathroom to use as needed will be worthwhile. (AginginPlace.org 2022)

Many remodeling and design considerations exist for anyone who intends to remain in their home as they age. Sometimes, this means completely changing an existing idea of a space's design to accommodate future needs. From something as simple as adding sensor lights to the area, or adding another bathroom, be sure to have a clear picture of your wants and needs in a bathroom design. (Agingin-Place.org 2022)

Bathroom Design

Bathroom Design: Do It Now or Later? Planning For The Future

One of the questions you might ask yourself is… "when should I remodel my main ensuite bathroom"? Make sure you can afford to remodel the bathroom to the point where it is usable. If you're limited on funds or time, you may need to leave parts of your project for later (paint, adding a new modern light fixture, or a new vanity countertop). There is time to do things now and in the future. The key is to be as prepared now before needs change. (AginginPlace.org 2022)

Perhaps an illness, accident, or another aspect of aging has affected your safety or those that allow access to the bathroom and need to be addressed now. Making the doorway wider, enlarging the room, and rearranging the layout for people using walkers and wheelchairs should take priority (and be remodeled first). These involve plumbing and electrical, installing grab bars, and a tub or shower that is easy and safer. (AginginPlace.org 2022)

S afety and Convenience Are Both Important

The ability to move quickly, safely, and conveniently in every part of the bathroom is essential. Falling in the shower, bathtub, or any part of the bathroom can be a frightening and physically devastating experience, and much time can lapse before anyone can help. (AginginPlace.org 2022)

A First Floor Accessible Bathroom

A first-floor accessible bathroom is convenient in a home with two or more floors. A bathroom on the first floor is suitable for visitors and essential for anyone age in place. Remember that the first-floor bathroom must be accessible, which means a more prominent space, which in turn, is safer and easier to use. (AginginPlace.org 2022)

The Bathroom Door

Bathroom doors must be wide enough (at least 36 inches) to accommodate a person in a wheelchair or who uses a walker, cane, or crutches. Since doors come in standard sizes, ensure the door size is big enough to accommodate a wheelchair in the future. A bathroom with a wide door will be accessible. (AginginPlace.org 2022)

I recommend you install a barn or pocket door instead of a "traditional" swing door to open up the space for anyone in a wheelchair or using a walker.

Extra Room for Wheelchair or Walker

It is not just the door that needs extra clearance. The bathroom needs to be big enough to be safely and effectively used by someone using a walker, wheelchair, or any other aid. There must be enough room to transfer to the toilet tub or shower and turn around without hitting walls. Think about these clearance issues to help provide safety and comfort. (AginginPlace.org 2022)

* * *

Tubs and Showers

A Step-In Tub

Bathtubs are not an issue for most young people, but getting in and out of one may be risky. Lifting a foot up and over the tub edge and maintaining the balance required can become problematic later. Others may prefer a stand-alone shower. (AginginPlace.org 2022)

If a step-in tub is wanted, be sure that it can accommodate needs, such as providing a place to sit down. Consider the height of the tub edge, a curtain, or a sliding door, and what can make the space inside safer. Look at how to enter and exit the tub and make that process more stable. Choose a tub with a textured bottom to avoid slipping and sliding. Install grab bars to provide stability and make entering and exiting a step-in tub easier if your balance is not strong. (AginginPlace.org 2022)

A Walk-In-Tub

If a step-in tub will not work, but a tub is wanted, a walk-in tub might be right. Walk-in tubs have a watertight seal door for easy entry and exit. Walk-in tubs provide the benefit of sitting down in a bathtub, relaxing, and helping ease aches and pains. These tubs have a handheld shower head attached, making washing easier. Many walk-in tubs are affordable, shorter than a standard bathtub, and fit in a smaller space (like a first-floor bathroom if needed). (Aging-inPlace.org 2022)

Roll-in Shower

Then there are roll-in shower options with no edge to roll a walker, wheelchair, or transfer chair right in. This makes getting in and out very easy and reduces the risk of tripping over the edge of a step-in shower. (AginginPlace.org 2022)

Showering

Portable Seat or a Built-in Bench

Water-proof seats, stools, and benches can be used in a shower or tub as a built-in feature or portable choice. The choice depends on several factors, the available space, whether parts are built-in to the tub or shower, and the need to take the seat from one place to another. A moveable chair or bench makes sense, so anyone can enter and leave the shower or tub more easily. In other cases, having a built-in bench may be better to make transfers easier. (Agingin-Place.org 2022)

The only problem with this choice is that specific future issues and options are unknown now. A built-in and portable bench can be the way to go if space is available. Thus providing the highest number of choices possible as needs change over time. (AginginPlace.org 2022)

Removable and Adjustable Shower Heads

Not all shower heads are equal. Some are standard sprays, while other sprays offer a lot more options. Choosing a shower head that allows a selection of sprays in the future helps reduce the chances that changes or upgrades are needed later. Rain heads can be suitable for washing when sitting down during a shower, but they may put too much water down, which might not be comfortable or safe as water can splash all over the floor. (AginginPlace.org 2022)

Consider a removable shower head with a hose that hooks into where the shower head would generally be, with the spray and adjustments on the other end. The shower head can move around where needed, and the spray type and strength can be changed, making it easy to wash and get clean while being safe. (AginginPlace.org 2022)

Toilet and Grab Bars

The Toilet

Most toilets are not set up to help people who need extra assistance. There are typical issues with toilets as people age. First, standing up and sitting down from the seat may become difficult. Second, most toilets are a standard height, but some toilets are a taller height. A taller toilet may make it easier (for some people) to sit down and get back up again. While sharing a bathroom with someone who does not need a taller toilet, adding an extra portable toilet seat to the 'regular' toilet seat to make it taller is a good compromise and makes things easier if and when extra help is needed. Third, some people have trouble accessing their bum to keep themselves as clean as they did when they were younger. An option to help stay clean is to add a bidet to the toilet seat. Having a bidet can help someone stay independent while reducing the risk of infection and related problems. (AginginPlace.org 2022)

Grab Bar Installation

Install grab bars by the toilet's side, in the shower or tub, or close by the shower or tub to remain. The grab bar beside the toilet helps to stand up and sit down. Bars made of metal are the best option; because they support more weight and are not difficult to clean. (AginginPlace.org 2022)

If a grab bar is not needed in the current design, building, or remodel of the main bathroom, put extra boards next to the toilet to reinforce the wall to make it easier to install grab bars later. Grab bars also make excellent towel holders if you don't need them to help you.

Small bars can fit into tight spaces, and much larger bars are used in showers and beside toilets when there is plenty of wall space. No matter what a bathroom design plan is, allow room for these bars. Creating the desired look without compromising style, security, and safety now or in the future; is possible. (AginginPlace.org 2022)

Consider all the places these bars or rails could go, and then go ahead and add them. There is less to worry about in the future since they will already be in place. (AginginPlace.org 2022)

A Bathroom Vanity

The Benefits and Drawbacks of a Double Vanity

There are several benefits to installing double sinks in the main bathroom. First is the issue of personal space. Installing a double vanity can also be great for the house's resale value. (Degnan, 2021)

While it is a convenient must-have for many couples, there are some tradeoffs. A double vanity will cost more, and two sets of fixtures will be needed. Two sinks will need plumbing; if space is an issue, a double vanity may not work proportionally in the design. (Degnan, 2021)

A typical single-sink basin is 17 to 19 inches wide. A double sink needs six feet or more to give both users enough space to maneuver. Furthermore, double vanity with two sinks has less counter space and storage. A double vanity will most likely not be an issue if other storage options are available in the room. (Degnan, 2021)

A Single Sink Bathroom Vanity

A single vanity offers additional counter space. If no extra square footage exists in the main bath, put a single sink with extra counter space into the bathroom. The space saved can make room for a massive roll-in shower, a separate soaking tub, and a separate shower. The sink also requires plumbing inside the vanity. A single sink costs less to plumb. With the money saved, there may be more budget for options like heated flooring, a new countertop, or upgrading tile choices. Plus, cleaning one sink is faster and easier than cleaning two. A single sink is an excellent option if you want more private storage options in the bathroom. (Degnan, 2021)

Roll-Under Sink and Countertop Height

In an ensuite bathroom, at least one of the vanities should offer space for someone in a wheelchair to roll under the sink. Doing things independently, like washing hands and brushing teeth, is much easier in a wheelchair when the vanity is open underneath and accessible. Make the countertop easy to reach in the back, and place the mirror in the perfect viewing spot, whether sitting or standing. (Aginginplace.org 2022)

Faucets, Cabinets, Shelves, and Other Stuff

All the fixtures and accessories in the main bathroom should properly work (as far as personal physical ability) when installing them. Will they work if circumstances change? Is the faucet still within reach when sitting in a wheelchair? Are things out of reach in cabinets? What about the shower shelves or cubbies? Are they reachable from the built-in bench? Focus on how to adjust fixtures and accessories to accommodate issues that may arise in the future. Lower cabinets and pull-down shelves make it much easier to reach items (faucets, controls in the tub, shower, and sink) if sitting in a wheelchair or using a walker. (AginginPlace.org 2022)

Master Bathroom Light

A well-lit bathroom is safer and more comfortable. When ceiling lights burn out, it may be hard and unsafe to reach the fixture to change the light bulb. A solution would be to install a few motion sensor lights that come on when someone enters and exits the bathroom; this saves electricity and reduces the chance of someone forgetting to turn a light off. (AginginPlace.org 2022)

In addition to motion sensor lights, consider lowering the lights on the wall instead of having them shine from the ceiling; to reduce glare. There are many spaces where these lights will work well. It is worth considering lowering the lights to see and also being able to reach them to change a light bulb. (AginginPlace.org 2022)

Bathroom Floors, Mats, and Rugs

A bathroom mat should stick to the floor, so walkers and wheelchairs will not get caught on it. Some bathrooms are not suitable for rugs and carpets. Even the best options can still get caught up in a wheelchair or a walker, making them more frustrating than helpful and causing a risk of falling. The tighter the space, the better off it may be with a more suitable flooring product (instead of a rug) that will not get too slippery if some water gets onto the floor. (AginginPlace.org 2022)

In this chapter, I talked about ways to design an ensuite main bedroom so you can age in place safely and efficiently. I wrote about some remodeling aspects, the aspects that should be done now, and what can be done in the future. I write about safety, having space to move around, and the importance of having a bathroom on the first floor of your home.

I also wrote about the width of the door, tubs, toilets, showers, benches, and grab bars. Finally, I wrote about vanities, faucets, cabinets, shelves, lights, and rugs.

In the next chapter, you will learn how to make other areas in the home accessible to you as you age in place.

10

NEVER SUFFER FROM LACK OF ACCESSIBILITY IN OTHER AREAS IN THE HOME AGAIN

There are other areas in a home that must be thought of when getting older. These spaces are guest bedrooms, bedroom closets, guest bathroom(s), an office, and eating/dining areas.

Bedrooms

Living with other people, visitors staying overnight, or living in a multi-generational home, one must think about having at least one additional bedroom in a home. Ensure that a bedroom is for a person in a wheelchair or who may need extra space. The bedroom dimensions should be at least 13 by 10'. There should be at least a 5-foot turning radius on one side of the bed. The bed should have a clear space underneath the frame in case extra medical equipment needs to be used to help (a patient lift). The overall height should be no more than 22" inches from floor to top of the mattress to ensure safe transfers if needed.

A dresser in the room should have no more than 60 inches tall. The nightstands should be sturdy. An outlet must be by the nightstand and hide cords to reduce falls.

There should be no throw rugs in the room unless they are adequately secured or there is carpet on the floor.

Guest Bedroom(s) Closet

A standard "traditional" guest bedroom closet is wide enough for two double doors equaling a 60-72 inch doorway clearance.

Suppose the guest bedroom has a 'walk-in' closet. The closet should have a 36-inch door at least 5 feet wide and 5 feet deep. Of course, bigger is better if this closet's secondary use is for extra storage. I will offer the same advice for designing a guest bedroom closet, as I stated in designing the main bedroom closet. A sliding door, barn door, pocket door, or even a fold-out door will add style to the room. Installing a lever-style door knob or pull handle on the door will make it easy to open.

In either case, hang at least one clothes bar 32 inches off the floor, in part of the closet. Make sure some of the storage shelves are also accessible. It is a good idea not to store many items on the floor because of access issues (hard to bend over or in the way).

Guest Full Bathrooms

At least one guest bathroom must be accessible to all home guests. A 5-foot turning radius, a toilet by a reinforced wall (to install a grab bar in the future), and a roll-under vanity are ideal things to include in this bathroom. Including a roll-in shower and linen closet in a guest bathroom is a terrific idea, too.

Guest half bathroom

If having a fully accessible guest bathroom is not attainable for now. A fully accessible half-bathroom may be an option. This bathroom does not need to be as spacious as a 'full' bathroom, as it usually has a toilet and a vanity. An excellent accessible half-bathroom is 5 feet by 7 feet if the room does not have a 'swing open' type of door. If the bathroom door is a "swing open" type, a great accessible half bathroom is 6 feet by 8 feet. A smaller wheelchair-accessible bathroom must have a pocket or barn door.

For this bathroom to be wheelchair accessible, a toilet must be installed by a reinforced wall for grab bar placement in the future. Installing a roll-under vanity is ideal. This bathroom also needs adequate lighting, easy-to-use switches, and accessories.

. . .

Office

Having an office in a home is also a benefit to the homeowner. If there is not enough space to dedicate a separate room for office space, incorporating an area in a bedroom or laundry space will work. Ensure enough space to include the essentials (roll-under desk, filing cabinet, shelves, etc.).

Another idea is to have a sofa or a Murphy-style bed in the office; that way, the room can have the dual purpose of also being a guest bedroom. If the office space can also become an extra guest bedroom, ensure that there will be enough space for a nightstand, a lamp, and a small closet, for storage.

Dining Areas

In the past, there was a room specifically for formal dining. Current trends are to forgo a "traditional" dining room and have space to eat in the kitchen. Regardless of the table location, ensure freedom around a table to sit safely and comfortably.

. . .

A Possible Rental Unit

Another current trend is to have a space in or close to the 'main' house as a rental option. This space can be an excellent option for some people who need extra income or extra help in the future. It is a great idea to add a kitchenette, laundry space, a bedroom, and of course, a bathroom to add appeal to this space. A caregiver can use the area for their own needs and still be close if assistance is required. Although, one does need to make a safe, informed decision when choosing this option.

In this chapter, I talked about the other areas of a home. I wrote about having at least one extra bedroom with a closet and a fully accessible bathroom in a home. I also wrote about how to make a half-bath accessible if needed. I also wrote about dining space and designing an office to double as a guest bedroom.

I also wrote about having a rental space and items to include and the possibility of a caregiver utilizing that space in the future.

In the next chapter, you will learn how to make a laundry room accessible as you age.

11

DOES YOUR CURRENT LAUNDRY ROOM LAYOUT STINK? HERE IS WHAT TO DO

Ahhh, finally, one of the last main rooms to consider when designing a home to age safely in place.

According to research from AgingInPlace.org (2022e), you should never underestimate the challenge of doing laundry. The laundry room must be safe, convenient, and easy to access. Creating an accessible laundry room is not simple. When re-designing a new laundry room layout, the room has to accommodate appliances, be conveniently located, and be organized. The following laundry room design advice will showcase how to maintain independence when doing laundry. AgingInPlace.org (2022e)

· · ·

The Location of The Laundry Room

For you, the days of lugging a laundry basket up or down stairs may no longer be safe or effective. The best place for a laundry room is preferably on the home's main level, making it accessible to most people. Choose a big enough area in the house that anyone can access. Avoiding hallway or structural obstacles while accessing your laundry room is better. Locate the main laundry room close to where you generate the dirtiest clothes, typically the bedroom(s). (AgingInPlace.org. 2022e)

Selecting a Washer & Dryer

Find appliances that will minimize the effort of doing laundry. Find a washer/dryer combination that will prevent any strain from lifting laundry from the washer to the dryer. Sometimes the best combination is a washer and dryer that are front loading, although sometimes, the best combo is a top-loading washer. (AgingInPlace.org. 2022e)

If you have neck or back problems, put both the washer and dryer on a pedestal, or consider placing the dryer between 10 and 15 inches above the floor; and leaving the washer on the floor. Having one or two of these machines raised off the floor will help you do your laundry, eliminating the need to bend over, and the control panel will be easier to see. (Aging-InPlace.org. 2022e)

Even if your eyesight is good now, laundry can be hazardous if you have trouble seeing in the future. A dryer set incorrectly could leave clothes in too long, at too high a temperature, risking a fire. Leaving clothes in a washer for too long could damage your clothes or, at the very least, waste energy if you choose the wrong setting. (AgingInPlace.org. 2022e)

Purchase a dryer and a washer with dial or digital controls that are easy to see. There are even some washers and dryers that can give their users information verbally. If the display is digital, ensure the screen is bright or adjustable to reduce strain on the eyes. A newer washing machine may be able to determine water level, cycle time, and other features making the devices more accessible for anyone to use regardless of age or ability. (AgingInPlace.org. 2022e)

The Laundry Room Layout

After choosing the room location and appliances, the next step is to organize the laundry room. The goal is to maximize space and minimize hazards when doing laundry. Everything (appliances and cabinets) should be visible when entering a laundry room. The best place for a washer and dryer is away from the door and against a wall. Wall or base cabinets should be close to the appliances. Place a laundry basket for dirty clothes next to the washer and a drying rack next to the dryer. (AgingInPlace.org. 2022e)

. . .

Flooring Options for the Laundry Room

Remember safety, budget, and specific mobility issues before installing the laundry room floor. If you choose a tile or hardwood floor, be careful if/when adding rugs and secure them to the ground to lower the risk of slipping. (AgingInPlace.org. 2022e)

Laundry Room Lighting, Switches, and Window

Lighting in a laundry room needs to be bright and easy to access. The best option is to install LED light bulbs into the ceiling lights. LED light bulbs last longer, consume less energy than traditional bulbs, and need to be changed a lot less frequently. (AgingInPlace.org. 2022e)

Install light switches that are easy to operate by fist or elbow if someone has their hands full or can not use their hands for some reason. Light switches need to be installed 36 inches from the floor to ensure easy access for anyone needing to reach them. (AgingInPlace.org. 2022e)

Besides electric lights, try to have a window in the laundry room to provide natural lighting. A window is good for physical and mental health, provides good ventilation, fresh air, and sunshine, and one can even do laundry with the lights off. ((AgingInPlace.org. 2022e)

. . .

Laundry Sink

A sink in the laundry room can improve the washing process if clothes or linens need to be cleaned by hand. Your priority should be ensuring the sink is easy to use; the space below provides easier access for a person in a wheelchair or using a walker. You must maintain the ability to turn the water on and off regardless of future skills, so a faucet must be easy to use with minimal force. A sink with a large basin provides more room to wash items. The single large basin helps clean the sink of the debris and grime in corners. (AgingInPlace.org. 2022e)

Install a motion-sensor faucet that turns on the water. A motion-activated faucet is also usable by children, anyone with limited mobility range of motion issues, people with dirty hands from gardening, and people with a hard time hearing or seeing. The best part is that the faucet will turn off automatically, so you don't have to worry. (AgingIn-Place.org. 2022e)

Setting up Counters and Other Work Spaces

Ensure that your laundry room has an area to fold clothes, rest items, and iron clothing. Choosing a separate countertop at the right height makes working in the laundry room safer and more accessible. A countertop must not block the door or the way to the washing machine and dryer and should be close to the dryer, allowing quick move dry clothes onto it for folding or ironing. Please choose a different color for the countertop from the color of the wall, floor, and appliances so it is easier to see. (AgingInPlace.org. 2022e)

Laundry Cabinets

Convenient access to essential laundry items is necessary. Cabinets are among the most common places to store detergent, fabric softener, and other things. Besides the location of the cabinets in a laundry room, the cabinets must be safe and accessible. In laundry rooms, cabinets are placed above the washer and dryer and on the floor (base cabinets) if space allows. (AgingInPlace.org. 2022e)

Upper Cabinets

Cabinets above the washer and dryer allow you to use the wall space above, but they can pose safety and efficiency issues and become. Placing cabinets above a washer and dryer increases the risk of spilling laundry detergent if it is located in an upper cabinet. If you have upper cabinets, store heavier, awkward items on the lowest shelves, reserving higher shelves for items rarely needed. (AgingInPlace.org. 2022e)

. . .

Base Cabinets

When placing cabinets next to the washer and dryer, if spills happen, the less likely you will get whatever you are spilling in your eyes or mouth if stored in a base cabinet. On the other hand, placing cabinets beside a washer and dryer take up room on the ground and give you less space to move around. However, you may hurt your back when bending down to access a needed object stored in them. Ensure the cabinets have easy-to-open handles instead of knobs, as handles are easier to open for someone with finger and hand dexterity issues. (AgingInPlace.org. 2022e)

Additional Storage

If there is not enough room for cabinets in your laundry room AgingInPlace.org. (2022e) suggests using the following options for storage:

- **Use Collapsible Shelves** to put laundry detergent, an iron, and other equipment on temporarily while doing laundry. When the laundry is done, collapse the shelves to avoid bumping into them again when entering the laundry room. (AgingInPlace.org. 2022e)

- **A Roll-Out Shelf** will help to maximize space by putting essential items on the shelf so the entire laundry room will be convenient and accessible. Such shelves are helpful for small and heavy objects that might be hazardous if stored in overhead cabinets. (AgingInPlace.org. 2022e)

- **Lazy Susans–** a lazy susan underneath a table or countertop helps store tall items you need to access.

- **Storage Bins–** Consider using storage bins for large, heavy items that would not fit most cabinets and shelves. Containers keep things safe from moisture or debris on the floor. They can be moved around the room and stacked as needed. Be careful about stacking heavy bins on top of each other. Removing a container from the stack may be dangerous, tip over, and create a falling hazard. (AgingInPlace.org. 2022e)

Making Ironing Safe and Easy

Ironing presents a unique challenge for many people looking to age in place. Traditional ironing boards are difficult to set up. They can become hard to operate when developing mobility issues, such as arthritis or loss of strength. To make ironing easy, install an ironing board that folds down from the wall. (AgingInPlace.org. 2022e)

Laundry Room Ventilation

AginginPlace.org (2022e) recommends having a fan in the laundry room. A fan provides several key benefits, including improving the room's air quality, delivering consistent comfort in the room no matter how long it takes, and a fan may help dry the laundry faster.

- **Improving Air Quality**– keeping a fan running while doing laundry helps to ventilate and freshen the air in the room. Air quality is critically important when exposure to poor air quality can worsen allergies, other health conditions, and respiratory problems.

- **Providing Consistent Comfort**– A fan in the laundry room will help you feel comfortable while doing laundry, no matter how long it takes.

- **Drying Efficiency**– when using an indoor drying rack to dry laundry, a fan helps it to dry more quickly.

Humidity Concerns

To reduce the humidity in the room, if you have a "traditional" dryer, ensure it is vented to the outside. Periodically check the pipes that run to the washing machine and sink for leaks. If humidity is still a problem, install a dehumidifier in the room. (AgingInPlace.org. 2022e)

Tips on Air Drying

An indoor drying rack, clothesline, or hanging clothes rod is a popular choice in your home, no matter where you happen to live. Whatever your reason for wanting an indoor drying option, There are several options for you, including:

- **Drying Racks**– People love their indoor drying racks almost as much as their outdoor ones. The frames are light and portable and can move to the middle of the laundry room or another space. An indoor drying rack makes drying delicate clothes easier. Just put away the drying rack when not using it, so it will not be in the way. (AgingInPlace.org. 2022e)

- **Wall-mounted Clotheslines**– A framed clothesline installed on the wall next to the dryer will make transferring clean wet clothes directly onto it to dry easier. This drying rack provides plenty of room to hang clothes without blocking the way. (AgingInPlace.org. 2022e)

How you air dry your laundry is your choice; adding a drying rack gives you greater flexibility to safely dry a wide range of items. (AgingInPlace.org. 2022e)

The Laundry Basket

By choosing the right type of laundry basket, you can make doing laundry easier. AginginPlace.org (2022e) recommends getting a laundry basket on wheels. Wheels make it easy to roll the basket, instead of carrying a heavy laundry basket, from room to room. Suppose your bedroom, bathroom, and exercise space are not close together. In that case, it is far more convenient to wheel a laundry basket to each location than to keep separate laundry baskets in each room. If the floor becomes slippery, a wheeled laundry basket can be used for support, although it should never replace a traditional walker.

Some Final Tips

- **Labeling:** To stay organized, it is a great idea to label bins, baskets, jars, and other essential items. Large clear letters and color-coding labels make it much easier to see the letters on the labels in the future. (AgingInPlace.org. 2022e)

- **Disposal:** One of the most common hazards in the laundry room is empty bottles. You must dispose of laundry detergent, fabric softener, or bleach correctly, safely, and efficiently. Before putting them in the recycling bin, wash the empty containers, so harmful chemicals do not spill when taking them out to a recycling bin. (AgingInPlace.org. 2022e)

- **Detergents:** It is essential to ensure that laundry detergent is easy to use. Traditional detergent bottles, which require you to pour the liquid, are heavy and could get hard to handle if you develop arthritis, mobility, or strength issues. If your laundry detergent spills, clean it up immediately to avoid slipping on the floor and injuring yourself. For this reason, you might want to store laundry detergent in an 'easy to use' bottle with a nozzle on the bottom, allowing the liquid to be poured into a cup. Alternatively, the use of detergent pods may be safer and more convenient for older folks to use. However, these tend to be more expensive. (AgingInPlace.org. 2022e)

- **Scheduling:** Once you have optimized the convenience and safety of your laundry room, you may be surprised by the next essential step: put your laundry on a schedule. (AgingInPlace.org. 2022e)

As you age, the loss of smell or memory may make it harder to tell when to wash your clothes and linens. Your dirty laundry may pile up, leading to health, safety, and quality of life concerns. You may not have those problems now, but aging in place requires planning. The earlier you develop a laundry routine, the easier it is to keep to it no matter what happens. Specific scheduling will vary based on your individual needs. In general, try to do laundry at least once every two weeks. If you pick the same day of the week to do your laundry, you're more likely to remember it. You can also set digital reminders on your phone and computer and more advanced laundry machines. (AgingInPlace.org. 2022e)

We all want to live independently, regardless of our time of life. Taking steps to address your laundry rooms' accessibility and usefulness can help you be as independent as possible for as long as possible. (AgingIn-Place.org. 2022e)

In this chapter, I wrote about ways to design a laundry room so you can age in place safely and efficiently. I write about safety, location, selecting a washer and dryer, the layout of the room, and safe flooring. I also wrote about laundry room lighting, light switches, and the importance of natural lighting from windows.

. . .

Next was the benefit of having a sink in the laundry room, faucets, countertop height, and color. I wrote about the different cabinets and storage options.

Then, I wrote about how to iron clothes safely, room ventilation, and humidity, and gave tips on how to air dry clothing.

Finally, I wrote about a great laundry basket option, labeling items, easy detergent options, how to dispose of empty containers, and creating a schedule to do laundry.

In the next chapter, you will learn how home automation and other technology will help you as you age in place.

PART IV

HELPFUL ELEMENTS TO HELP YOU AGE IN PLACE

After describing how to age in place safely in multiple areas in a home, the following three chapters describe resources that will help you remain independent in your home as long as possible. They are home automation, finding professionals and organizations, and financial assistance available to people in the United States of America.

12

WHAT IS HOME AUTOMATION AND HOW DOES IT WORK?

A home automation system can help create a home that is comfortable, enjoyable, and safer to live in. Home automation uses technology to help with housework or any household activity. (Age In Place, 2019)

What is Home Automation?

Home automation provides remote or automatic control of devices in a home, possible responses, and a notification of an event happening in a home sent to an intelligent machine. (Age In Place, 2019)

Notifications sent to a smart device (tablet, smartphone, system control iPad, television, or another device) allow control of individual settings, including creating new event triggers, responses, and schedules. (Age In Place, 2019)

When the doorbell rings, an app on a cell phone shows who is at the door. A home automation device can send a notification (to you) if a pipe in the home breaks, an intruder is near your home, or a package is on your porch while you are away from home, turn lights on at night, and open a garage door. A home automation system can also provide family members with important safety information on another loved one's activity, such as ensuring a loved one eats or take medications and even sending notifications when a person gets out of bed. (Age In Place, 2019)

What is home automation: Basic information

The researchers from Age In Place (2019) describe the components of a home automation system as a controller (the brain), the devices that can be 'activated' by the system, an interface (keypad, smartphone, tablet, or TV) and the system's network (how to interact between the device and controller).

. . .

Do-It-Yourself or have it professionally Installed?

The good news about a home automation system is that there are many options, but where to start? Home automation systems are available from various manufacturers and sold online and through many stores. The system can be purchased as a whole (each package geared towards specific types of automation functionality) or as individual components if the price is a consideration. (Age In Place, 2019)

Depending on the technology used and the system's complexity, there may be a steep learning curve. A trained and certified professional home automation installer (can help plan the automation system design, suggest options, and even help set up the system. Hiring a professional may be the best choice if you are not confident about the technology or the different functions available. (Age In Place, 2019)

Before you start

As with most things, a good plan is where to start. Research and figure out what functions a home automation system can perform. Talk with a few installers about the technology and possibilities. Alternatively, get advice from friends or family who have home automation systems. What do they like about their plans? What do they dislike? What would they have done differently? ((Age In Place, 2019)

. . .

What Home Automation Can Do for You

There also are other, more enjoyable aspects to home automation. For instance, you can control your home theater system and home appliances that are connected to the system and have your favorite songs flow from speakers from room to room. (Age In Place, 2019)

Senior safety is one of the most significant benefits of a home automation system. An alarm can be set off if someone breaks a window or opens a door when they should not. Cameras can be connected to the system outside the house or CO2/Radon gas monitoring and fire alarms. From basic home safety and security to event, audio, and video monitoring, these systems can help older people remain safe in their homes. (Age In Place, 2019)

Of course, there are other benefits, such as saving money on electricity with an automated thermostat (and being able to adjust the thermostat from anywhere via a smartphone or tablet), the convenience of being able to turn lights on or off (or appliances) from anywhere in the house, phone call monitoring and management, video conferencing, visual weather alerts and even opening and closing shades or curtains. The possibilities are endless. (Age In Place, 2019)

. . .

Remaining Independent

A home automation system will help you remain independent in your home. We all forget things as we age; many people experience forgetfulness to a greater degree. This 'forgetfulness' can lead to serious safety issues, so having an excellent way to remember and remind seniors about essential things is crucial. (Age In Place, 2019)

Assistive or Adaptive Technology

An assistive device or adaptive technology is any electronic or non-digital product that helps people with challenges remain independent. Many assistive technology apps exist for you who choose to age in place. Smartphones have made a significant difference in home safety and security concerns. Keep an open mind; the gadgets, apps, and assistive devices can be surprisingly easy to use. (Bellport, 2021)

Memory

Help With Organization and Routine

Natural forgetfulness and significant life changes (like retirement) might throw off a sense of routine.

Sometimes, forgetting things and disorientation is severe in people with dementia or Alzheimer's. Assistive technology can help structure time and activities and benefit people with these conditions. Smartphones and other intelligent (AI) devices can help people with daily reminder prompts. (Bellport, 2021)

Other specific assistive tools can address particular reminder needs. For instance, a digital calendar offers each day's date, time, and weather information. An automatic pill dispenser can control medication dosage and release medication at certain times, increasing consistency and preventing an accidental overdose. Some smartphone apps allow someone to set up a daily visual prompt; so a loved one can check off the medications taken. (Bellport, 2021)

Losing keys, a phone, a wallet, or a purse is easy. Putting a location device on the object will prevent the thing from getting lost. The information on the location device is programmed into a smartphone app if the item ever goes missing. (Bellport, 2021)

Voice Recordings

A voice recording can be programmed into an AI device connected to your system that provides step-by-step instructions for specific activities (like dressing) is particularly impressive. (Bellport, 2021)

For instance, someone could program an alarm for 10 AM. An Artificial Intelligent device can give audio instructions that say, "Time to get dressed. Pull the top drawer handle of the dresser open. Take out one shirt, pants, and pair of socks...." (Bellport, 2021)

The following can be enhanced with home automation.

A Telecare system

A telecare system can detect a change in routine (not getting out of bed), a fall, or an unlocked or open door. These systems also include personal alarms that a loved one wears. Emergency services and contacts can be alerted at the touch of a button if there is a problem. (Bellport, 2021)

GPS trackers

GPS trackers can be life savers for those with dementia or Alzheimer's who wander away from home and forget how to return. They can be a wristband or hidden in shoe insoles that are hard to remove. Many vehicles have GPS trackers installed in them. (Bellport, 2021)

Appliance Monitors.

Similarly, monitors for appliances can send alerts when a refrigerator or freezer door is open, a stove/oven is left on, and even shut off electrical or gas devices automatically if they detect smoke. (Bellport, 2021)

Home Security System

A home security system should not be complex or alarming. A doorbell will alert homeowners to anybody approaching their front door by looking at a video of the guest. As awful as it seems that somebody could take advantage of an older adult, especially one with memory loss, it does happen. Because of that, this is an essential addition for most aging people who live alone. Sometimes the mere presence of a visible alarm system is enough to deter unsavory folks. (Bellport, 2021)

In this chapter, I wrote about how home automation may help you at home. I explained a home automation system, its components, and who could install it for you. Next, I explained how tech could help you with everyday tasks, safety, and safety responses. Third, I explained how technology could help with organization tasks, daily routines, memory aids, medication reminders, item locators, personal safety, and appliance monitors. Finally, I explained how a general alarm system could help you remain safe in your home.

In the next chapter, you will learn how to find professional help to help you age in place.

13

THE ULTIMATE GUIDE FOR FINDING PROFESSIONAL HELP AS YOU AGE IN PLACE

As time goes by, aging-in-place changes are designed to custom-fit a home to a homeowner's needs. Finding a building specialist to help age in place is getting easier. (Bawden, 2020)

Certified Aging-in-Place Specialist (CAPS) program

One such specialist is called A Certified Aging-in-Place Specialist (CAPS). This program is a nationwide initiative that provides educational training to construction and design professionals through the National Association of Home Builders and AARP. The CAPS program design principles focus on elegant, enriching, and barrier-free environments. The CAPS program connects professionals with homeowners that need services on an increasing basis. All active professionals who become Certified Aging-in-Place

Specialists (CAPS) are in the Professionals with Home Building Designations directory. A person with a CAPS credential is a professional who helps modify or build a home designed to last a lifetime. A Certified Aging-in-Place Specialist must take business training, maintain certifications through education, and follow a code of ethics. (Bawden, 2020)

In addition, a Certified Aging-in-Place Specialist helps to make a home more "visitable" for visitors, family members, and future homeowners. These people will benefit from an accessible home even if the current homeowner does need an accessible home. (National Association of Home Builders, 2022)

Finding Local Resources to Help

Wanting to age in place means choosing to stay in *a specific* home in a particular neighborhood in *a specific* city as long as the services or assistance needed are available. If a bad fall occurs and hinders one ability to drive independently, personal care assistance in many rural areas may not be available. Unfortunately, in some rural areas, that means moving for the first time. Services such as in-home care, transportation, home help, and maintenance are available in other areas. (Hager, 2018d)

Companies that provide personal support and assistance do seem more available in areas where people aged 65 and older make up more than 20% of the population. Given how the current systems, methods, and institutions of care are set up, the number of people in that age group will not be able to be well-supported by many communities. There will be trouble in a community with little to no services, no new programs, and services, or a poor job of integrating private-pay services and products from local businesses. (Hager, 2018d)

Resources in Age-Friendly Communities

The World Health Organization (WHO) states that age-friendly environments "are free from physical and social barriers and are supported by policies, services, products, and technologies." Age-friendly communities are neighborhoods with elected offices, nonprofit organizations, universities, and businesses. Churches and local nonprofit organizations may provide services or referrals. These environments promote health and enable people to continue participating in activities they enjoy and value. WHO notes that age-friendly policies anticipate and respond to aging-related needs and preferences and promote inclusion in all areas of community life. (The Rural Health Information Hub, 2021)

Many community resources help older adults carry out critical everyday activities such as bathing or cooking. These resources include community businesses, nonprofit organizations, care managers, senior centers, and local area agencies on aging. Tribal organizations, provincial, state, and federal government resources, friends, family, and neighbors can also help provide services to those who want to remain at home. (The Rural Health Information Hub, 2021)

Luckily, some small businesses provide concierge, errand, and personal assistant services in local areas for seniors.

Concierge services are about providing for customers' needs and building experiences. Some concierge services include help with transportation, shopping, shipping, travel companionship, money management, handling insurance or medical disputes, companion shopping or recreation activities, etc. (Hager, 2018a)

. . .

Errand services may include helping with mailing, shipping, or delivering packages, light grocery shopping, drop-off services (dry cleaning, prescriptions, gifts), Returns (store purchases), Meal delivery, personal shopping, and many more. (Hager, 2018b)

A Personal Assistant helps an older adult with day-to-day activities. A personal assistant may: help plan and make travel arrangements and home organization tasks, arrange home services (cleaning, maintenance, lawn care), assist with paperwork, shopping, hobbies, organizing, planning, and preparing for social activities or arrange for vehicle maintenance or other services. (Hager, 2018c)

Community Services That Can Help

The Rural Health Information Hub (2021) explains other community services to help people live independently. These include:

- Personal care – help with bathing, toileting, dressing, eating, and grooming.

· · ·

- Other services: housekeeping, help with shopping, laundry, and yard work.

- Nutrition services deliver meals to individuals at home or provide meals to community centers. Nutrition service providers may educate, screen, assess needs, and counsel others.

- A medical physician can prescribe home health medical services for people who need short-term help or have chronic medical conditions or disabilities.

- A Care coordinator helps make referrals to other service providers, helps schedule appointments, and communicates information between the patient, providers, and other organizations. (The Rural Health Information Hub, 2021)

Other people who can help are family caregivers, paid skilled medical care workers, community businesses, nonprofit organizations, senior centers, and tribal organizations. (The Rural Health Information Hub, 2021)

. . .

State Services That Can Help

The following state initiatives to help older rural adults remain in their communities are stated below. (The Rural Health Information Hub, 2021)

SASH® (Support and Services at Home) in Vermont utilizes affordable housing communities that promote independent living to help provide care and services to adults and individuals with disabilities. (The Rural Health Information Hub, 2021)

The Arkansas ARcare Aging Well Outreach Network provides fall prevention assessments, transportation to appointments, medication management, and exercise opportunities for residents over 50 in Cross County, Arkansas. (The Rural Health Information Hub, 2021)

Neighborhood Program of All-Inclusive Care for the Elderly (PACE), run by the East Boston Neighborhood Health Center, provides care and support for adults in East Boston. The program provides medical, social, recreation, rehabilitation, home care, transportation to each

PACE Center, and medical appointments. (East Boston Neighborhood Health Center, 2022)

For more information about home and community support and services available in rural areas, please refer to the RHIhub's Rural Aging in Place Toolkit. (The Rural Health Information Hub, 2021)

In this chapter, I talked about the definition of A Certified Aging-in-Place Specialist and the national initiative to provide education to construction and design professionals. I wrote about the many community and state services resources available to those who age in place.

In the next chapter, you will learn about the funding resources available to you as you age in place.

14

WHAT EVERYONE MUST KNOW ABOUT THE FINANCIAL ASSISTANCE AVAILABLE FOR ACCESSIBLE HOME MODIFICATIONS

The economics of modifications to aging-in-place make sense. Compare the cost of an assisted-living facility ($60,000 a year) to the cost of widening a bathroom door, installing a grab bar, and adding a roll-in shower ($6,000 to $15,000) once. (Bawden, 2020)

Many sources of assistance are available to help people make home modifications; it is essential to distinguish between the types of assistance available. Low-Interest Loans, Home Improvement Grants, Non-Profit Organizations or Charities, and Equipment Loans. (Paying For Senior Care, 2021)

1. **Low-Interest Loans** – Some governmental organizations offer low-interest loans for home modifications. (Paying For Senior Care, 2021)

2. **Home Improvement Grants** are a one-time "gift" for a specific home improvement. (Paying For Senior Care, 2021)

3. **Non-Profit Organizations or Charities** offer free labor to make a home improvement. Materials are not covered. An example is building a ramp for a wheelchair. (Paying For Senior Care, 2021)

4. **Equipment Loans** – are loaned out by organizations for as long as the person needs them. An example is a portable wheelchair ramp. (Paying For Senior Care, 2021)

Medicare's / Medicare Advantage Benefits for Home Modifications

Medicare Part B will pay an occupational therapist to make a home evaluation to determine what changes are required. The Occupational therapist then recommends the changes to the doctor. Then Medicare may pay for a medically necessary device (or home modification) that a doctor prescribes. Medicare will only pay for the hardware required for home modification(s), not labor. (Paying For Senior Care, 2021)

Most states have Home and Community-Based Services (HCBS) Waivers that offer services to help individuals remain at home; Medicaid programs or Medicaid State Plans fund that. These waivers and programs that pay for home modifications increase an individual's ability to live independently. Each program has different eligibility requirements and benefits. (Paying For Senior Care, 2021)

The Department of Veterans Affairs provides three programs for veterans that make home modifications to accommodate veterans' combat disabilities or disabilities resulting from aging. Those programs are the Specially Adapted Housing (SAH) grant, The Special Housing Adaptation (SHA) grant, and the Home Improvement and Structural Alteration (HISA) benefit. (Paying for Senior Care, 2022)

· · ·

Specially Adapted Housing – SAH Grant

The SAH grant provides financial resources to veterans to make their homes accessible. This assistance is only for veterans with combat disabilities affecting limb loss or function or who have sustained severe burns; that become worse with age and require the use of a wheelchair. This grant application has no time frame limitation. (Paying for Senior Care, 2022)

Eligibility

Veterans must have a combat disability resulting in the loss of, or function, of a limb, blindness, or severe burns. (Paying for Senior Care, 2022)

Benefits and Limits

The maximum limit for 2022 is $101,754. This figure is adjusted yearly based on the cost of construction. Veterans temporarily living in a family member's home can benefit up to $40,983, known as a Temporary Residence Adaptation (TRA) grant. (Paying for Senior Care, 2022)

Special Housing Adaptation – SHA Grant

This grant is to provide home modifications for veterans with service-related disabilities to continue to live independently. This grant can help an eligible person buy an existing modified home. (Paying for Senior Care, 2022)

Eligibility

To be eligible, a veteran must be blind in both eyes, have lost the use of both arms, lost their abilities relating to a burn, or have a significant respiratory injury. (Paying for Senior Care, 2022)

Benefits and Limits

The 2022 maximum grant benefit amount is $20,387. If the applicant lives in a relative's home, the maximum benefit is $7,318. (Paying for Senior Care, 2022)

The Home Improvement and Structural Alteration – (HISA) Benefit

The HISA benefit is a financial resource available to disabled veterans needing to make home modifications that are medically necessary to improve access and mobility, mainly to help them use a bathroom. This benefit may cover the cost of adding handrails, ramps, electrical outlets, medical equipment installation, roll-in showers, and widening of doorways. The veteran's disability does not have to be from military service, although veterans who obtain a service disability are eligible for a higher benefit. (Paying for Senior Care, 2022)

Eligibility

Veterans must have a Veterans Affairs (V.A.) doctor's prescription stating the diagnosis and medical reason for needing home modification. The veteran does not need to own the home. However, they must have the homeowner's permission, as indicated by a signed and notarized statement. (Paying for Senior Care, 2022)

Benefits and Limits

In 2022, the maximum HISA benefit lifetime limit for veterans whose disability is not from military service is $2,000. For veterans with service-connected disabilities, the lifetime limit is $6,800. (Paying for Senior Care, 2022)

Application Process

As stated above, veterans must have a medical prescription that displays their name, address, phone number, and the diagnosis resulting in the need for a home modification, what home modification is needed, and one bid for the cost of the job. (Paying for Senior Care, 2022)

Veterans Directed Home and Community-Based Services (VDC) program provides financial assistance to help veterans remain in their homes. It gives the veterans discretion to use the funds as they see fit. (Paying for Senior Care, 2022)

Acceptable use of funds is making home modifications to accommodate a disability regardless of whether their disability is from prior military service. (Paying For Senior Care, 2021)

Veterans pensions, such as Aid & Attendance, offer a one-time bonus for "unreimbursed medical expenses." To cover the cost of a home modification that is a medical necessity, a veteran who receives a pension can get a temporary increase in benefits. Finally, the Rebuilding Together program called 'Heroes At Home' offers home modification assistance-labor and materials to U.S. veterans. (Paying For Senior Care, 2021)

. . .

Non-Medicaid Government Assistance

Many state governments and agencies have programs to help with home modifications. The Department of Housing and Urban Development (HUD) distributes Home Improvement Loans, and the U.S. Department of Agriculture (USDA) has Rural Repair and Rehabilitation Grants. Many states offer assistance programs offering financial assistance and support services to help home-owners remain at home.

(Paying For Senior Care, 2021)

HUD Loans

Non-profit organizations can apply for HUD loans to help older low-income adults modify a home, allowing them "to age in place with dignity." (Smith, 2022)

U.S. Department of Housing and Urban Development has $15 million to help older Americans through the Older Adult Home Modification Program. According to HUD, the money will help non-profit organizations, housing authorities, and state and local governments with programs to make safe and functional home modifications meet the needs of low-income elderly homeowners. (Smith, 2022)

The home modification program aims to enable low-income elderly persons to make low-cost, high-impact home modifications that reduce falling risk, improve safety and increase accessibility. (Smith, 2022)

Examples of home modifications include installing grab bars, a stair railing, lever-handled door handles, faucets, a temporary ramp(s). Home improvements may include a transfer bench for a tub/shower, a hand-held shower head, raised toilet seat, furniture risers for chairs and sofas, and non-slip safety strips for showers or stairs. (Smith, 2022)

HUD's Notice of Funding Opportunity (NOFO) is available online. Eligible applicants can apply for funds through Grants.gov. (Smith, 2022)

USDA Rural Repair and Rehabilitation Grants for the Elderly

. . .

To participate in the USDA Rural Development Loan and Grant program, to be eligible for the loan, homeowners must be 18. To qualify for the grant, homeowners must be 62. Applicants must live in a rural area (less than 10,000 people) of the country for both the loan and the grant. This program also has income limits. Individuals must have an annual income of less than 50% of the area's median income. (Paying for Senior Care, 2020a)

There is a limit on non-retirement assets, meaning that within 90 days, assets are cash. In a house where a person (under the age of 62) lives, the limit is $15,000. In a house where a person (older than 62) lives, the asset limit is $20,000. (Paying for Senior Care, 2020a)

USDA Rural Repair and Rehabilitation Grant Benefits and Limits

The lifetime maximum of the USDA Rural Development Grant amount is $7,500. The grant must be for home repairs and improvements to benefit the health and safety of the occupants of the home. In addition, within three years of receiving the grant and selling the house, the USDA can collect repayment from the recipient's home sale. (Paying for Senior Care, 2020a)

. . .

Non-Profit and Foundation Assistance

Many non-profit organizations offer financial aid or volunteer labor assistance to help with home modifications. (Paying For Senior Care, 2021)

Rebuilding Together

Rebuilding Together is a national non-profit organization with several programs and community-building projects that help low-income families, veterans, and the elderly remain at home and age by providing free home modifications services.

Rebuilding Together has nearly 150 affiliates nationwide. (Paying for Senior Care, 2020b)

This coalition of non-profit organizations, volunteers, and corporate agencies offers three primary programs: Safe at Home Program, Heroes at Home Program, and National Rebuilding Day. (Paying for Senior Care, 2020b)

. . .

Safe at Home

This program is for low-income seniors and families who own their homes and require assistance maintaining them in livable conditions or whose disabilities require minor home modifications to enable them to continue residing in their homes. The organization's volunteers help install a ramp, handrails, toilet riser, shower chair, special lighting, and smoke detector and help with other safety improvements. (Paying for Senior Care, 2020b)

Applications are accepted and reviewed by local Rebuilding Together chapters. Eligibility criteria are also determined locally. Typically, the organization focuses on lower-income households. (Paying for Senior Care, 2020b)

Heroes at Home

This program is for veterans, their families, caregivers, widow, and widowers. The program modifies homes to make them accessible to veterans in wheelchairs. The home modifications include the construction of a ramp and remodeling bathrooms, hallways, and kitchens to help veterans maintain independence. (Paying for Senior Care, 2020b)

Applications

This program is a partnership between Rebuilding Together and Sears Holdings. It is open to honorably discharged veterans who are homeowners and need home modifications to maintain their independence. Rebuilding Together local affiliates provide services, and applications are accepted and reviewed locally. (Paying for Senior Care, 2020b)

National Rebuilding Day

National Rebuilding Day program occurs on one day or a few days in April, when thousands of volunteers work on home modifications across the country. The program services low-income families, seniors, and individuals with disabilities. Improvements and changes are limited to those that can be done in one day and managed by volunteers. For example, installing handrails might be viable, while remodeling a bathroom might be seen as too extensive an effort. (Paying for Senior Care, 2020b)

Applications

Applications are accepted and reviewed by local *Rebuilding Together* affiliates. Many chapters allow applicants to file their applications from June to October, although some extend as late as February. Additionally, some chapters expanded their projects to include a second day. Check with a Rebuilding Together affiliate for more information about an area's National Rebuilding Day program. (Paying for Senior Care, 2020b)

Other Financial Options for Home Modifications

Reverse mortgages are another option for home modifications. A reverse mortgage enables a senior (or their spouse) to live at home for a minimum of several years. Homeowners should know that the cost of home modifications, or a portion of the cost, is tax deductible. (Paying For Senior Care, 2021)

. . .

Labor Cost versus Materials and the Reason It Matters.

A home modification cost can range depending on the type of modification; many people need to realize that the cost can and should have two components: the price of labor and the cost of materials. An important distinction because some materials for home modifications can be classified as durable medical equipment (DME) and therefore covered by financial assistance. For example, when adding a stair lift, there is the cost of the chair, the sliding track, and the installation. The stair lift may be classified as durable medical equipment, while the cost to have it installed is labor. (Paying For Senior Care & 2021)

The Rural Health Information Hub provides examples of organizations and grant programs that have funded aging-in-place.

- **Older Americans Act**

This federal program includes funding the Community Innovations for Aging in Place Initiative, which awards grants to community organizations that identify strategies to support aging. (The Rural Health Information Hub, 2019)

- ### Health Resources Services Administration (HRSA)

HRSA funds provided through the Federal Office of Rural Health Policy Community program support a person's ability to age in place. These healthcare services are available to uninsured, isolated, and medically vulnerable adults. (The Rural Health Information Hub, 2019)

- ### The U.S. Department of Health and Human Services

Provide grants and contracts to states, territories, tribes, and non-government agencies. (The Rural Health Information Hub, 2019)

- ### Village to Village Network

The Village to Village Network is a non-profit network of organizations that help coordinate and deliver services and support within their community. (The Rural Health Information Hub, 2019)

- **<u>Naturally, Occurring Retirement Community Supportive Service Programs</u> (NORC-SSP)** in New York State

Provide support to maximize programs and health services that support aging in place. Through NORC's Health Indicators Initiative, aging-in-place supporters can offer resources to help high-risk clients. (The Rural Health Information Hub, 2019)

In this chapter, I talked about the funding resources available to you as you age in place in The United States of America.

The third part discussed how to design specific areas around and in your home so you will never have to move. The fourth part of this book states the different types of professionals, services, and resources available to you. The fourth part of this book points out additional funding resources available to you. In this book's fifth and final part, I showcase the other two books I wrote that are available for purchase.

Essential Things To Remember From This Book

Why would you want to Age In Place? Why take my advice?

What is Universal Design? Who is Universal home Design For?

Why should you incorporate universal design into your home? Who benefits from Universal Design?

What Is Aging in Place? What Does an Aging-In-Place Renovation Mean?

How to design your home (room by room) for you to Age-In-Place.

Who are the professionals who specialize in Aging-in-Place?

How to get help from professionals who specialize in Aging-in-place?

What is a Certified Aging-in-Place Specialist (CAPS)?

What are the home automation options that can help you Age-In-Place?

What are the current technology options that can help you Age-In-Place?

The current services and resources to help you Age-In-Place.

The existing financial resources that help you Age-In-Place.

Thanks for buying this book; I hope you have enjoyed it. Now you can incorporate everything you have learned from this book into practice."

In this book, I promised to show you how to create an accessible home; you never have to leave by incorporating aspects of universal design, aging in place, and accessible design. Have I succeeded? Please let me know in the 'comment section' where you purchased this book.

PART V

MY OTHER BOOKS

DESIGNING YOUR FOREVER HOME:

Designing Your Forever Home: 116 Things to Think About When Designing Your Forever Home

There are many things to think about when building a new house. Read this book to help you think about everything involved with designing a new home.

HUMAN AFTER ALL

Human After All

by Kate Margaret Bigalk

This book of poetry is about my experiences as a woman in a wheelchair and the universal themes that influence the lives of everyone.

My poems can put words to feelings that don't seem to have any conventional definition. These poems capture ordinary moments of life into something either funny, beautiful, or something that touches the heart.

HUMAN AFTER ALL

Human After All

by Kate Margaret Bigalk

This book of poetry is about my experiences as a woman in a wheelchair and the universal themes that influence the lives of everyone.

My poems can put words to feelings that don't seem to have any conventional definition. These poems capture ordinary moments of life into something either funny, beautiful, or something that touches the heart.

REFERENCES

1. Advocate Construction. (2022). METAL ROOF VS. SHINGLE ROOF: THE PROS AND CONS OF EACH. https://www.advocateconstruction.com/metal-shingle-roof/

2. Age In Place, (2022a). Carport Parking & Garage Ideas for Aging in Place. Age in Place. https://ageinplace.com/at-home/aging-in-place-home-ideas/aging-in-place-home-remodeling-garage-carports-parking/

3. Aging In Place, (2022b). Home Exterior Ideas for Aging in Place. Age in Place. https://ageinplace.com/at-home/aging-in-place-home-ideas/aging-in-place-home-remodeling-exterior/

4. Age In Place. (2019, July 21). Aging in Place Communities. Aging in Place. https://ageinplace.com/aging-in-place-basics/community/

5. AgingInPlace.org (2022, July 17). What To Do When You Redo Your Bathroom. https://aginginplace.org/what-to-do-when-you-redo-your-bathroom/

6. AgingInPlace.org (2022a, July 18). Important Updates And Modifications For The Bedroom. Aging in Place. https://aginginplace.org/aging-in-place-important-updates-and-modifications-for-the-bedroom/

7. AgingInPlace (2022b, July 18). Kitchen Of The Future: Remodeling For Comfortable Aging In Place. https://aginginplace.org/kitchen-of-the-future-remodeling-for-comfortable-aging-in-place/

8. AgingInPlace. (2022c, July 18). Making Your Entryway Safer. Aging in Place. https://aginginplace.org/5-ways-to-make-your-entryway-safer/

9. AgingInPlace.org. (2022d, July 18). Aging In Place? Consider A Living Room Update For Safety And Security. https://aginginplace.org/aging-in-place-consider-a-living-room-update-for-safety-and-security/

10. AgingInPlace.org. (2022e, July 18). Remodeling Tips For A Safe, Convenient Laundry Room. https://aginginplace.org/age-in-place-autonomy-remodeling-tips-for-a-safe-convenient-laundry-room/

11. AIPatHome.com (2014, April). The Indivo Kitchen. Retrieved September 29, 2022, from https://www.aipathome.com/aboutus/news/newsletters/2014-04-bulletin.htm

12. Bawden, D. (2020, January 8). What is Design for Independent Living? National Association of Home Builders. https://www.nahb.org/education-and-events/education/designations/certified-aging-in-place-specialist-caps/Additional-Resources/What-is-Design-for-Independent-Living

13. Bellport, L. (2021). The Ultimate Guide to Assistive Technology for the Elderly. Live in Place Designs. https://liveinplacedesigns.com/the-ultimate-guide-to-assistive-technology-for-the-elderly/

14. Bernal, R. (2022, August 26). 10 Best Power Recliners (Fall 2022) - Which One to Buy? ReclinerLand. https://www.reclinerland.com/best-power-recliner/

15. Bowen, S. (2021b, March 23). 9 Types of Dishwashers You Should Know. Avantela Home. https://avantela.com/home/appliance/types-of-dishwashers/

16. ChildProofingExperts.com & The International Association for Child Safety. (2020, February 1). TV Safety - *Don't forget to Anchor! | Childproofingexperts.com.* ChildProofingExperts.com. https://www.childproofingexperts.com/tv-safety-3/

17. Degnan, A. (2021, March 8). Dual or Single Bowl Vanity: Is One Or Two Master Bathroom Sinks Best? Degnan Design-Build-Remodel. https://degnandesignbuildremodel.com/blog/2019/11/21/dual-or-single-bowl-vanity-is-one-or-two-master-bathroom-sinks-best#%7E:text=While%20many%20homeowners%20like%20a%20double%20sink%20in,vanity%20offers%20other%20benefits%2C%20like%20additional%20counter%20space.

18. East Boston Neighborhood Health Center. (2022, July 18). Are your health care needs changing? https://neighborhoodpace.org/pe/

19. Everstead. (2020, June 13). Universal Design: A Home Designed for All. https://everstead.com/universal-design-a-home-designed-for-all/

20. Fregenal, R. (2019, September 7). The Resale Value of an Accessible Home. Houseopedia. http://web.archive.org/web/20220215060134/https://www.houseopedia.com/resale-value-accessible-home

21. Fregenal (2019b). A Home Safe Room in Time of Storm Danger. https://www.houseopedia.com/home-safe-room-time-storm-danger

22. Fregenal, R. (2021, January 5). Want to Age in Place? "Universal Design" is Crucial. Houseopedia. https://www.houseopedia.com/age-in-place-universal-design-crucial

23. Garage Door Repair Peachtree City. (2022). Different Types of Garage Door Opener Remotes | Peachtree City, GA. https://www.garagedoorrepairpeachtreecity.com/types-of-garage-door-opener-remotes

24. Ganea, S. (2022, April 20). Custom Countertop Height Kitchens – Defying The Standards. Homedit. https://www.homedit.com/countertop-height/

25. H, A. (2020, August 2). Garage Door Repairs Make it Easier For Seniors to Age at Home. styleourlife.com. https://styleourlife.com/garage-door-repairs-make-it-easier-for-seniors-to-age-at-home/

26. Hager, M. (2018a, December 28). Concierge Services For Seniors. Aging in Place. https://ageinplace.com/aging-in-place-professionals/concierge-services-seniors/

27. Hager, M. (2018b, December 28). Errand Services for Seniors. Aging in Place. https://ageinplace.com/aging-in-place-professionals/errand-services-seniors/

28. Hager, M. (2018c, December 28). Personal Assistant for Seniors. Aging in Place. https://ageinplace.com/aging-in-place-professionals/personal-assistant-seniors/

29. Hager, M. (2018d, December 28). Why Is Aging in Place Important for All Business Owners? Aging in Place. https://ageinplace.com/aging-in-place-professionals/aging-place-important-every-business-owner/

30. Heimerdinger, B. (2021, October 7). ACCESSIBLE ENVIRONMENTS: WHY INCLUSIVE SPACES BENEFIT US ALL. FingerReader.org. https://fingerreader.org/why-inclusive-spaces-benefit-us-all/

31. HOMEBUILDING / REMODELING GUIDE. (2022). Building A New House? Never Want To Move Again? A List Of Universal Design Features Your Home Needs! [Must-Haves For Aging In Place]. Retrieved August 29, 2022, from https://homebuilding.thefuntimesguide.com/aging-in-place-universal-design/

32. Homestratosphere's Editorial Staff & Writers. (2021a, January 15). Sensor Faucets (Pros and Cons). Home Stratosphere. https://www.homestratosphere.com/sensor-faucets/

33. Homestratosphere's Editorial Staff & Writers. (2021b, September 20). The 8 Main Types of Kitchen Faucets. Home Stratosphere. https://www.homestratosphere.com/kitchen-faucet-types/

34. Lentz, S. (2022, July 6). The Single Handle Faucet (What are the Benefits?). Home Stratosphere. https://www.homestratosphere.com/single-handle-faucet/

35. MacLachlan M, Cho HY, Clarke M, et al. 2018. Report of the systematic review on potential benefits of accessible home environments for people with functional impairments. In: WHO Housing and Health Guidelines. Geneva: World Health Organization; https://www.ncbi.nlm.nih.gov/books/NBK535292/

36. National Association of Home Builders. (2022). Certified Aging-in-Place Specialist (CAPS). https://www.nahb.org/education-and-events/education/designations/certified-aging-in-place-specialist-caps

37. Paying for Senior Care. (2020a, September 14). USDA Rural Repair and Rehabilitation Grants for the Elderly. https://www.payingforseniorcare.com/home-modifications/usda-rural-repair-grant

38. Paying for Senior Care. (2020b, October 9). Rebuilding Together (Christmas In April) Home Modification Projects. https://www.payingforseniorcare.com/home-modifications/rebuilding-together

39. Paying For Senior Care. (2021, January 19). Home Modifications for the Elderly: Loans, Grants & Financial Aid. Paying for Senior Care. https://www.payingforseniorcare.com/home-modifications/how-to-pay-for-home-mods

40. Paying for Senior Care. (2022, September 14). SAH, SHA & HISA Programs: Veterans Assistance for Home Modifications. https://www.-

payingforseniorcare.com/home-modifications/veterans-sah-sha-hisa-grants

41. Renovations, T. R. S. B. T. B. (2018, March 6). 15 tips for nailing your kitchen location & layout. https://www.realestate.com.au/lifestyle/15-tips-for-nailing-your-kitchen-location-layout/

42. Saladino, A. (2022). 15 TYPES OF KITCHEN SINKS FOR EVERY KITCHEN DESIGN. Kitchen Cabinet Kings. https://kitchencabinetkings.com/ideas/types-of-kitchen-sinks

43. Stone, J. (2022). 30+ Different Types of Refrigerators (with Photos). Upgraded Home. https://upgradedhome.com/types-of-refrigerators/

44. Smith, K. (2022, August 22). HUD Grants: $15M for Older Adults Aging in Place. Florida Realtors. https://www.floridarealtors.org/news-media/news-articles/2022/08/hud-grants-15m-older-adults-aging-place

45. The Lighting Research Center, Rensselaer Polytechnic Institute, & Figueiro, M. (2001). Lighting the Way: A Key to Independence. Rensselaer Polytechnic Institute. https://www.lrc.rpi.edu/programs/light-Health/AARP/pdf/AARPbook2.pdf

46. The Rural Health Information Hub. (2019, June 4). Program Funding. https://www.ruralhealthinfo.org/toolkits/aging/6/funding

47. The Rural Health Information Hub. (2021, April 8). Community Supports for Rural Aging in Place and Independent Living. https://www.ruralhealthinfo.org/topics/community-living

48. Truehold. (2022, September 30). How Can Universal Design Benefit You? Universal Design Perks. https://www.truehold.com/post/how-can-universal-design-benefit-you

49. Ullman, M. (2021, June 19). Types of Gutters to Consider for Your Home. Bob Vila. https://www.bobvila.com/articles/types-of-rain-gutters/

50. Walker, S. (2022, May 2). Certified Aging in Place Specialist: What Do They Do and How to Become One? RespectCareGivers. https://respect-caregivers.org/certified-aging-in-place-specialist/

51. Whalen, M. (2022, September 26). Aging In Place- Kate Bigalk's Universal Design Project. Fillmore County Journal, 2–4. http://fillmorecountyjour-nal.com/2022-fall-home-garden/?fbclid=IwAR2Uzjlxhq4A26i8-Abs9T4-ZlHTS6ROEZEvaqWERVbE1FBg3SILrmpTtWhA

www.ingramcontent.com/pod-product-compliance
Lightning Source LLC
Chambersburg PA
CBHW060916140726
47996CB00001B/271